John Preston Campbell

The Poetical Works of John Preston Campbell

John Preston Campbell

The Poetical Works of John Preston Campbell

ISBN/EAN: 9783337427856

Printed in Europe, USA, Canada, Australia, Japan

Cover: Foto ©Thomas Meinert / pixelio.de

More available books at **www.hansebooks.com**

THE

POETICAL WORKS

OF

John Preston Campbell.

TOPEKA, KANSAS:
GEO. W. CRANE & CO., PRINTERS AND BINDERS.
1885.

Entered according to act of Congress, in the year 1885, by
JOHN PRESTON CAMPBELL,
In the office of the Librarian of Congress, at Washington, D. C.

PREFACE.

IN venturing to collect and publish in book form, the scattered children of my muse, I do so with great hesitancy, knowing that to launch these tender nurslings of my affection upon the unknown sea of criticism may endanger their lives. But whether they shall reach the harbor of fame in safety, or sink into oblivion and forgetfulness beneath the scathing words and imperial frown of some self-constituted critic, I shall be content in knowing that even the sarcasm of a Swift cannot deprive me of the pleasant hours spent in the the production of the lines which I now offer to the public.

Crude and imperfect as they are, still the just criticism of a generous public, and the touch of maturer manhood, may yet correct their faults.

J. P. C.

JANUARY 2, 1885.

NOTICE TO THE PUBLIC.

Several of these poems have been published at intervals in some of the periodicals of the country, under the name of Arthur E. Silverthorn, a mere fancy of my own, perhaps without justification.

All rights, however, are reserved by the author.

JOHN PRESTON CAMPBELL.

TO THE MEMORY

OF

LUELLA ANNALEE EDSON,

THIS VOLUME IS

AFFECTIONATELY DEDICATED

BY THE AUTHOR.

CONTENTS.

	PAGE
Proem,	9
Those Hills of God,	11
The Valley of Visions,	17
The Lady of Lodel,	45
The Minstrel and the Maid,	55
Irene Imogene,	61
The Peri's Pardon,	69
The Fountain of Youth,	71
Death in the Rear,	73
Elza Dreve,	77
A Hut in the Forest,	81
Those Celestial Bells,	85
The Chimney Sweep,	89
The Mists of the Morning,	93
Despair,	95
The Stream of Time,	101
The Immortal Masters,	105
The Harp of a Hand That's Still,	109
Celestial Melodies of the Air,	113
Love and Time,	117
The Poet's Departed Shades,	121
The Shadows of the Night,	123
Darts of Death,	125
A Poet of a Golden Age,	129
The Sea of Galilee,	135
We Come and Go,	137

CONTENTS.

	PAGE.
THE HEADLESS HORSEMAN,	143
ANELBE AND THE ANGEL,	149
SIR ROBERT GIVES HAD SEVEN WIVES,	155
MILDRED,	171
TWO ANGELS,	175
ANNALEE,	183
ORPHEUS AND EURYDICE,	189
ST. PETER AT THE GATE,	195
THE LAND OF LOVE,	199
LIFE'S BATTLES,	205
BRAVE-BORN SOULS,	207
THERE IS NO UNBELIEF,	209
HOW A LARK CHEERED A DROOPING SOUL,	212
FLAKES OF SNOW,	214
THE ORDERLY'S RIDE,	216
EVENTIDE IN THE RHINELAND,	219
AWAY TO-NIGHT,	221
MIDNIGHT ON THE BATTLE FIELD,	222
SITTING AT THE STILE,	224
OUR SLEEPING DEAD,	226
HOPE ON,	228
BURIED YEARS,	230
MABEL MAY,	233
NO EARTHLY VOICE,	235
NEARING THE END,	237
DEATH AND THE FAIRY FAY,	239
THE PARADISE LIGHT,	240
FAIRY SHORE,	243

PROEM.

Children of my fancy,
   Whatever your fate may be,
Whether you reach the harbor
   Or perish in the sea:
Memories fond will ever come back to me,
   Of the early time,
When first I penned
   The thought sublime,
Of those mountains grand,
Eternal still as heaven's command;
   And of the later day,
I sought to pen a longer
   And a more enduring lay.

Whoever the critic be,
Whatever fault he may see,
   Each word and line
Is dear to my muse and me;
   And blest memories may entwine
   Round thoughts, lofty and sublime,
Through the association of sympathy,
   Which the heartless critic
May never see,

As by pen and rule,
He follows the formal methods
  Of the school;
Marching on life's parade,
  With gilded bow and shaft,
Against each literati arrayed,
  Striving only to shine
By the utter annihilation
  Of some friendless rhymer's rhyme.

THOSE HILLS OF GOD.

NOTE.

This poem was suggested to the author while sitting on a peak of the Rocky Mountains one afternoon, near the " Garden of the Gods." The subdued carol of birds, the sounding of waterfalls, and the sublime scenery of mountain peaks against the azure sky, stretching away into infinity, made impressions upon my youthful mind which I had never realized before.

C.

THOSE HILLS OF GOD.

Those hills of God,
Those sentinels of time,
Rock-ribbed and ancient,
Formed by a hand divine.

Tho' covered with snow
In Autumn's glow,
Or bleak and bare,
Those sentinels of air,
Point heavenward everywhere.

Those hills of God,
All bare and broad,
Towering so high,
Their summits seem
To reach the sky.

Those hills of God,
Those peaks of light,
Immortal gleam
Through all the night.

Those hills of God,
That beck and bow
At the Eternal's nod,
Oh, let my song applaud!

Those hills of God,
Those sentinels grand,
Eternal are
As heaven's command.

Those hills of God,
Where the ancient Shepherd
All unshod,
Sought the lost one
Fainting on the sod.

Those hills of God,
And towers sublime;
Upon their summit's line,
Mortal eye may see
The footprints of the Deity.

Those hills of God,
And soulless stones,
Are supporting now
Bright, viewless thrones.

THOSE HILLS OF GOD.

Those hills of God,
And towers of might,
Angels visit
On their earthward flight.

From those hills of God,
Mortal may,
With eye supreme,
Catch a heavenly gleam
Of the thitherward shore unseen;

While round their summits go,
Winging from this world below,
Amid a glorious, golden glow,
Many a little cherub sprite,
On that mysterious flight
To worlds of endless light.

THE VALLEY OF VISIONS.

THE VALLEY OF VISIONS.

PART FIRST.

A Mysterious Realm.

I.

There is a valley,
   Deep, mystical, queer,
With a sort of an alley,
   Leading to the castle of fear.
Located somewhere
   Between this floating ball,
And a city celestial, fair,
   Where the apples of paradise fall.

II.

Neither river nor strand
   Breaks on the view,
But a kind of mystified land
   As you wend this valley through;
Where a deep brooding gloom
   Hangs dimly around,
Both at night and noon
   In the depths of this desert profound.

III.

In this region so dim,
  So lonely remote,
The fancy may swim,
  And swimming float,
Through leagues of dead space;
  Where never a living thing
Or one of the race
  May be seen on the wing.

IV.

Dim, distant and far,
  Vague, fathomless and cold,
Glimmers the ghost of a star
  Over this valley so old;
Like a somber lit ray
  Gilding the graves of the dead,
Or a gleam of the judgment day
  Breaking round the cold head.

V.

There fleshless phantoms stalk
  Upon the grassless wold,
And at the stride of Time doth mock,
  Whose touch is no longer cold.
In those undulating plains,
  Beyond the river of mists,

Where eternal stillness reigns
   And each one doeth as he lists.

VI.

By some transporting spell
   I entered this valley of visions,
While I in the flesh did dwell,
   Against my prior decisions.
But brave as I am,
   And solicitous to know,
I felt a sort of qualm
   About my being go.

VII.

But listen unto me
   And I'll tell to you,
Without favor or fee,
   That which I never knew
Till those regions I had trod,
   Ranged not by mortal man,
Beyond the domain of God,
   And Satan cloven shod.

VIII.

'Twas there I saw
   A shadowless shade,
Of wing and claw
   That naught divine e'er made;

Wrinkled, crinkled and grim,
  Limping lonely across the wold,
As if the distant ages dim
  On his frame had hold.

IX.

With scepter in his fleshless hand,
  And a sort of bearing brave,
He ruled the mystic land
  Beyond the Stygian wave;
And when he me beheld,
  He raised his withered cane;
Which had the twist and twirl of eld,
  And thus he spake in labored pain:

PART SECOND.

The Shadowless Shade.

I.

"What seekest thou,
  In this valley now?
Neither hell nor Heaven,
Hobgoblins, witches seven,
Nor the widow of Nain,
  With her hand of leaven,

Hath crossed this plain,
  Till from the flesh shriven.

II.

"I hold the key
  To this vale of mystery,
And at one sweep
Of my viewless wing,
I could around thee fling
An army of spectres gaunt,
That would tear thee limb from limb,
As they would an ant;
And hurl thee deep within
Darksome regions dim.

III.

"But thou seemest to be
  No common form of mortality,
And perchance may safely go
Through the land of mist and woe."

IV.

Whereat he waved his hand,
In gesture of command;
And there passed before my view,
  Myriads of weird things,

Some with claw and finger too,
   And others with wizen wings,
Indeed they were a motley company
That dwelt within the vale of mystery.

V.

They didn't laugh,
They didn't cry,
But a kind of mournful sigh
Swept the valley through;
As if some source of pain
Lay hidden beyond my view.

VI.

Then the shadowless shade,
Took me to his castle, made
With golden gilded tapestry,
Like that which decks
The moonlit lea,
Near a foam-crested sea.

VII.

The rooms were neither large nor small,
The ceilings did rise and fall
   At the wish and will of my guide,
Who showed those mysteries
   With high and haughty pride.

VIII.

A row of golden bells,
Hung round the emblazoned panels;
   Which lit each spacious room
Like death's feeble taper
   Burning dimly at the tomb.

IX.

The floor was inly laid
   With a transparent something,
By skilled phantisians made;
   And the furniture fine,
Had come from unknown workmen,
   Of the ether line,
And was loosely placed around;
Which moved without a sound,
As we wended on
   From room to room,
About that gilded castle
   In the valley of doom;
Which shadowy seems and queer
To one of the earthly sphere.

X.

From thence we cleft the ether line,
With mystic wings,
Which had been furnished,

By this guide of mine;
Till pausing on a golden boundary,
Thus he spoke to me:

XI.

"Mortal, this is the line
  Between my shaded realm,
  And just Alla's clime;
Thither thou canst not go,
Hither no rills of mercy flow;
No blest Peri wings its flight,
  Over this line so fair and bright.

XII.

"No sound or seraph crowned
  My dim retreat hath ever found.
In short, there is no interchange
  Between my viewless company,
And those who freely range
  Over the hills of sanctity."

PART THIRD.

The Invisible Line.

I.

From this spot we flew
  To an invisible line,
  Which dimly burned
With white and blue.
  It proved to be
  The dividing line,
  Between this valley
  And the dreadful mart,
Where the devils all free
Revel in sport and glee.

II.

In mystic speech, once more,
  With much meaning,
Or meaningless as before,
Thus spoke the stranger guide to me
Concerning this new found mystery:

III.

"Mortal! see'st thou that line,
　　Drawn between my realm
　And where the fires of hell shine?
　　'Tis the boundary set to be
　　The dead line to all eternity,
　　Between those dominions and me;
Beyond which none ever go
From this valley to the shades of woe;
　　And none from thence may come,
　　As the ages of eternity run.

IV.

"And were it not for this
All earth would be amiss,
Because my crippled sprites,
Would put out hell's lights
Which sometime gleam across the void
When they feel with weariness annoyed.

V.

"And as the devils do
Build up those fires anew,
They sometimes make
E'en my dominions quake,
With their thirstful wail
To make hell's minions quail.

VI.

"Indeed, sir, venturous one,
  Were it not for this line,
Hell's mighty legions
  Would with mine combine,
And march against just Alla, good,
  And tear from heaven
  Whate'er there is divine,
Which ages long hath stood.

VII.

"For they sometimes think
As the sulphurous wave they drink,
That Heaven's royal Prince
Hath laid too great a curse,
On his children of the universe.

VIII.

"But no foot may shun
The line by some mishap run,
Round this vale of mist,
When earth and ocean kist
The new creation's light,
At the dawning of day
From universal night.
When no weird thing
On foot or wing,

E'er woke an echo's swell
In the chaste dominions where I dwell.

IX.

"But I've heard whisper
    That a time will come,
When a form all heavenly, divine,
    Will about these wastes appear,
With vesture fair and fine,
    Bright, shining, clear,
And disperse the shadows
    Which I've assembled here,
With blast from a golden horn,
    When ushering in
The world's new morn.

X.

"Say, stranger, then,
    What thinkest thou
Will become of my secluded glen,
    And the shadowy hosts I've led
Ever since your Mother Earth
    Felt man's tread,
And went bounding into birth.
    Heaven won't want us there,
The decrepit and weird,
    Among the shining fair:

For we'd mar its holy joy
  And work the saints
Of glory foul annoy;
  In the land where always May,
Sheds her fragrant bloom
  And perfume gay,
On seraphs wreathed in flowers,
  Singing amid amaranthian bowers.

XI.

"Thou speakest not,
Thou stranger guest,
To this soul opprest.
Then go with me,
And thou shalt see
Souls more white than thine,
Deep penance doing
In the pit of purgatory,
With light divine o'erflowing."

PART FOURTH.

The Pit of Purgatory.

I.

Whereat he flew
Right onward through,
  Leagues of dead space,
And of wonderment, too:
  Leading me free,
As the billow-bounding sea,
  To a curious cavern's mouth,
In his dominions
  Farthermost south.
He slacked his pinions,
  Then, pointing to the pit, said he:
"Behold the festive fair of purgatory!"

II.

Within the pit I saw
Wretched shapes of awe,
Doing penance to atone,
With grief and groan,

For the sins of earth,
   From Father Adam given
At each succeeding birth,
   By the decree of Heaven.

III.

Sometimes frivolity and mirth,
   Swells high the chorus
Of voluptuousness,
   With music deep, sonorous;
Till the whirl of dizziness
   Overcomes the mind,
   In its giddy search to find,
Some pleasure in the bowl
   Of bitterness they drain,
In deep anguish of soul,
   Within the pit of pain.

IV.

'Twere long to tell
   What scenes I saw,
What there did dwell.
   For my vision, running out,
Reveled carelessly about,
   Through all that hidden place,
Never seen before
   By mortal face.

V.

There was suffering, yes,
Everything ran to excess:
In those regions dim,
Vagaries did float and swim.
And when a spirit came flitting, lean,
It seemed the apparition of a dream,
Or some shape of boding ill,
Turned loose in melancholy mood to kill.

VI.

There were spirits the length of a span,
And the brawny bones of man;
There were skulls scattered round;
   And ever and anon
A deep groaning sound,
   As if making moan for the decay
Silently working away,
   Crumbling to mold
Mortal bodies of gold:
   As if to wipe
From the catalogue of Time
   The last type
Of the form divine;
   In that fanciful clime
Which superstition hath built,
   On the martyred blood

Church persecution hath spilt,
  To pave the way to Heaven
For the redeemed and forgiven.

VI.

In fine, you might see,
In the pit of purgatory,
Any fleshless thing
With claw or wing,
With bone or groan,
With hollow eye or sunken face,
In attitudes of grace,
Doing penance and dole
For the peace of the soul,
By purgatorial light
Neither warm nor bright,
Where always night
Broods on the dreary waste;
And each moving thing,
Of claw or wing,
  Cuts the silent air
Where no man is king,
  Through the valley there.

VIII.

Oh, the imploring look,
  And sorrowful sigh

Those penitents took,
   As I passed them by.
On an archway bright,
   Emblazoned in letters of light
     With golden carvings nice,
I beheld these words
   Of strange device:
"Neither shadow nor shade
   May join the heavenly parade,
Till true penance it hath made.
This judgment, I,
The ruler of the sky,
Have on all things laid."

IX.

Much I marveled
That there should be,
Such dire decree
In the shadowy vale of mystery:
That artist could be found
In those dim dominions round,
Who could trace those letters free,
Like pencilings of the Deity.

X.

But there they were,
   Full shining forth

Without blot or blur,
   In a realm far
From earth or star,
Where shapes of misery are.

VI.

'Tis true, some vague tradition tells,
   Of a point or place
Where the departed dwells,
   Till they have gotten grace,
And sinless come,
   With angel face,
'Neath the rays of eternity's sun;
   Which guilds the holy hill of God,
   Where no polluted foot hath trod,
Or discord's grating jar,
Where all the loved and loving are.

XII.

And some old son of song,
With mumbling tongue
And manners bold,
Hath in chronicles told
That beyond the river Styx,
Remorse's golden needle pricks
The sleeping conscience to atone
For sins so ghastly grown.

By some mysterious right,
The fleshless soul
Keeps up an endless fight,
Till never spot or speck
Doth its whiteness deck.

PART FIFTH.

The Place of Skulls.

I.

From thence my guide
   Crossed a plain,
All wild and wide,
   Flowerless, fruitless;
O'er which no living thing
Did glide on foot or wing,
To the place of skulls
Thrown in at intervals;
Regardless of form or kind,
Brainless, bloodless, blind.
Indeed it was a ghastly scene
Which came over
The spirit of my dream.

II.

Skulls, skulls, skulls,
Of kings and conquerors,
Skulls of drones and warriors,
Of bright divines
And worshippers,
Skulls of lords and ladies gay,
Skulls of poverty stricken peasants, lay
Scattered round that mystic ground
On every hand.
As if some prodigious ban,
Of excommunication held
Them in that place;
    Like monumental stones,
Or mummies of the race
    Reared on dead men's bones.
By the superstitious light
    Made from their marrow,
Which serves to guide aright
    The robber chief,
In his hellish work at night,
    Through ways of grief;
As he smears with mortal blood,
The hands by just Alla given,
With which to earn an honest living.

III.

Awful, horrid things,
Without body, legs or wings;
Expressionless and void,
  Lifeless and null,
As a dull November day,
  Was each forsaken skull,
Mouldering where it lay;
  Waiting the sounding trump
Of the judgment day,
  To break the reign
Of universal stillness
  In that mysterious domain.

IV.

Thus to me again
Spoke the withered swain,
  Who was my guide around
The weird regions
  Of this mysterious ground:

V.

"Behold my dominions
Wild and wide,
Peopled with a race that's gone,
Who in their lifetime
Filled the world with song,

And moved the nations great,
With the cares of men and state,
Mere wrecks of manhood,
   Skeleton bones,
Who once with dignity stood
   Filling earth's thrones;
But yielding to the decree of fate,
Came in at the valley gate,
Never to go hence,
Till the thrill of life intense,
Shall fill these mortal bones,
With resurrection groans."

VI.

Ending thus he led me back,
Over the wondrous track,
From out that valley strange,
And wayward, winding range,
To the margin of this sphere,
   Watered by the rolling main,
With the single words,
   "Adieu, we meet again!"

VII.

Then away the specter flew,
   And left me in a region
Both wild and new.

Long I pondered on what I saw,
In the valley of visions,
  Beyond Nature's law;
Where neither God nor man
  Holdeth reign,
But some prodigious ban,
  Ruleth the plain,
Veiled in mystery quite,
And hid from mortal sight.

VIII.

This valley of visions wide,
  Is the midway station
Between Charon's tide,
  And yonder city fair,
  Built on nothing but the air,
  With golden winding stair.

IX.

Formless, phantom's strolls,
  Through the hidden valley
Of penitential souls,
  Away beyond earth's rim,
  Far, vague and dim
Through those regions
  Where wonderments begin,
  And shadows float and swim

Unreal, unearthly, strange,
Like moving sentinels
　Along eternity's range.

X.

'Tis a valley we
Shall one day see,
When the light of life grows dim,
And our senses swim,
And the cries of mourners dull our pain;
And we hear the boatman's loosened chain,
And the portals of eternity folds
　Forever round our vanishing souls.

THE LADY OF LODEL.

NOTE.

While visiting in the West one summer, the author frequently heard repeated the Indian legend of "The Lady of Lodel," which suggested the following lines. It seems from the tradition that this lady was a beautiful Indian queen, who feared death, and sought to guard against the approach of the grim shade by a fortification of her island, and a resort to arms; but in vain—hers was the fate of mortals. They still think, however, that her spirit hovers near the island, when tired of the sports of "The Happy Hunting Ground."

C.

THE LADY OF LODEL.

PART FIRST.

In a distant dell
I've heard the fairies tell,
At the evening curfew knell,
Of the Lady of Lodel,
   With her mirage clear;
All in the twilight hue,
And on the sparkling dew,
Forever plain to view,
   Lighting up the atmosphere.

This lady grand
Was queen of all the land,
Defended by an armed band,
Who guarded well her island strand
   'Gainst the reaper, Death;
For she was very fair,
With ringlets rich and rare,
Like some form of air,
   And would not yield her breath.

For many years,
Through joy and fears,
With her compeers,
'Gainst Death she rears
   Her fortress walls,
And sports the day
In pleasure's sway,
Nor thinks of passing away
   Till a croaking voice calls.

Then a grizzl'd shade
Strides across the glade
Through all her armed parade,
And touches this queenly maid
   With a hand of ice;
She feels the thrill
Of his fingers chill,
And yields to his iron will
   And quits her earthly paradise.

PART SECOND.

But her spirit may be seen
Like a fleshless queen,
Still sporting on the green
'Mid shade and shadows sheen;
   Changed from clay

To an airy thing
With beauteous wing,
Or some transparent fondling,
   By the imagination's play.

On moonlight nights,
Along the heights,
As eternity's lights
Guide viewless sprites,
   She may be seen,
Commanding the dead,
With a queenly tread,
Through realms of dread,
   With a fearless mien.

Her soldiers gone,
Parade upon the lawn,
Singing her dying song,
Through the day's declining dawn,
   With a sorrowful flow;
As if to condole
The woes of her soul,
In eternity's goal,
   While they marching go.

The traveler who strays
'Neath the moonbeam's rays,

Or on misty days,
Doth in horror gaze
　On her apparition there,
Haunting the island round
Like a soundless sound,
Floating from under ground
　Through all the ghostly air.

PART THIRD.

No hum of insect life,
Or din of busy strife,
Or breeze with fragrance rife,
Or song of toiling wife,
　Breaks on the ear;
No living thing
From bough to bough to spring,
On foot or wing,
　Is seen from far or near.

A death-like stillness stands
Spreading ghostly hands,
Over all the lady's lands,
Where viewless bands,
　Decked with vesture dim,

To mortal eye unseen,
Sport on the verdant green;
Where no reapers come to glean
   Round the island's mystic rim.

There on recurring times,
When withered witches lines
Their wild, weird rhymes,
And the bell of death chimes
   Its heart-breaking knell:
As some freed soul
Plunges into the fathomless goal
Of eternity's roll,
   For heaven or hell.

PART FOURTH.

'Tis said there came
A youth with brow of flame,
Who spoke the lady's name
With soft angelic strain,
   Saying, "Follow me
From your isle away
Through the gateway of day,
Into a brightening ray,
   For I'm the herald of eternity."

Then the lady with her train,
Cast one look of pain,
And spoke the angel's name,
And mounted up in flame,
   Athwart the heavens borne;
And with a favoring gale,
Out of sight did sail,
Beyond the rising veil,
   Into the beams of eternity's morn.

The island sunk from view
Like a transient dew,
Or a ship's drowning crew,
And oblivion round it drew,
   It's dusky wings;
Like a vapor chill
Seemed the abysmal void to fill
With gloom, more gloomy still,
   Wafted from deep hidden springs.

No ghost or goblin then,
No form or shape of men
Went through that dusky den;
All darkness to the human kin;
   Oblivion there held reign,
With undisputed might,
And no ray of light,

Flashed upon the night,
   Through all that dread domain.

Far away on high
Through the gateway of the sky,
Blinding to mortal eye,
Like a rocket shooting by,
   Burst a flood of light
Adown the dismal space,
From the lady's angel face
Bedecked with golden lace,
   By some seraph sprite.

Then she seemed to ride,
In the golden eventide,
On charger prancing wide,
Along the heavenly mountain side;
   Grown more glorious now,
Queen of a brighter land,
And a fairer strand,
Where death's cold hand,
   Shall never touch that angel brow.

THE MINSTREL AND THE MAID.

PART FIRST.

On a distant mountain side,
In the golden eventide,
'Neath the moonbeam's rays,
And a kind of lovelight haze:
Near a lake of amber shine,
Where the myrtle and the eglantine,
With mutual interlace
Beautify the lovely place,
Sat a minstrel and a maid
On the fragrant, flowery glade,
Talking each to each,
In mystic meaning speech,
Of the art that thrills,
At recurring intervals,
The soul with chords sublime,
With the holy flow of rhyme,
Touched by an immortal hand,
While journeying to the heavenly land;
And of the blushing morn
When true womanhood is born,

With the meek-eyed grace
Of an angel's in the face;
And of hope's bright charm
And the knell of death's alarm,
When the reaper's sickle keen,
With varied flash and sheen,
Sweeps unsparingly then,
In among the files of men,
Gathering the fairest flowers
From blooming meads and bowers,
And with relentless stride
Hurries them over the Stygian tide,
Away to some mystic glen
Beyond the river's hem.

While thus in talk,
A distant echo seemed to mock
Their varied speech,
As they were talking each to each;
'Twas thus the maiden then
Spake unto the grandest of men:

PART SECOND.

"Oh, minstrel whence thine art,
  That moves to life the throbbing heart,
  And at the touch of varied strains,
  Thrills with soul-tormenting pains?
  Oh, say, what mystic spell,
    Dear friend of mine,
  Enchants this beauteous dell,
    With thy notes divine?
What holy flow of soul
    From thy minstrel art
Doth round me roll
    From yon realm apart,
Destined to be
The eternal goal
    For this weary heart?"

The minstrel then replied,
With tender accents
Sitting by her side:

"Sweet maiden mild,
 More like angel
 Than earthly child,
 This art of mine
 Is the moving of a hand divine.
 The thrilling of these strings
 Is moved by angel wings,
 Poised in attitude to fly
 From earth to sky,
 With the penitential tear,
 Which flows so clear
 Over a sinner's cheek,
 Repentant, warm and meek,
 When some tender strain
 Moves the fount of sympathy again,
   Which for many years
 Hath frozen been
   By sin's soul-chilling tears."

"Oh, minstrel may the morn be fair
 That calls you yonder there,
 With your harp and bow
 From this world below,
 And may you sing
 On angelic wing,
 Your sweetest strain,
 Soft as falling rain,

To me sorrowing here,
As you cleave the ether clear
Upward to that wondrous sphere."

"Oh, maiden, cease your plaint,
Call me not a saint;
For I'm a man of sin,
With God, and heaven and all to win;
Though divinely gifted,
When the veil be lifted,
And yonder flood of light
Comes blinding to the mortal sight,
Many will be there,
Far more fair,
With a diviner art
To move the throbbing heart,
With ecstacy supreme,
Beyond the Stygian stream,
And the dreadful sweep
Of hell so dark and deep."

"Come, minstrel, play
Your sweetest lay,
Ere the stride of time
Enters this sunny clime,
Changing the fragrant bloom,
Like mantle of the tomb,

Black as dismal pall,
To break the cheer of all."

With that he touched the key
That woke his sweetest minstrelsy,
While amid the strings,
With viewless wings,
Love's fairies flit
Which the minstrel's face hath lit;
Then the current of his soul
Seemed in music to roll
Over the golden board,
Like a psalm of heaven poured
From ten thousand reeds,
Touched by angel hands above,
In the far-off lands of light and love.

And the minstrel's brow
Glowed with glory now,
As if some heavenly light,
Or meteor's bright celestral ray,
Broke round the musician,
While the immortal melody floated away
   On the night wind's air;
Echoed and reëchoed everywhere,
By invisible singers
   Singing round the golden stair.

IRENE IMOGENE.

I.

Lovely Irene Imogene
Was a Hindoo valley's queen,
In the distant days
When Oriental poets
Sang the praise
Of those amorous gods,
   Who left their sphere
To mix and mingle
   With mortals here.

II.

The subject of my song,
One glorious eventide,
Roamed the flowers among
By a streamlet's grassy side,
   Whose brillant sheen
Mirrored the mirage
   Of this peerless queen.

III.

When winging from some sphere
In the heavens far remote,
Out of the ether clear
A vision of splendor
Seemed to float,
   Borne on the zephyr's breath,
Over the way
   This maiden wandereth.

IV.

It was the god Ione,
Who reigned on a sapphire throne:
   But tiring of the sky
And the ritual of that realm
   Where time speeds slowly by,
This venturous god
   Earthward cast an eye,
Perchance some mortal
   Of the softer sex to spy,
With charms and intellect,
   Seraphic pure and high.
By some heavenly spell
To transmit from earthly shores,
To realms where dwell
   The gods of light alone,

Without one daughter of Eve
   To share the glory of their throne.

v.

While thus wandering he
Beheld the image fair,
Like some form of divinity
Mirrored in the water there,
   As if inviting him
To linger one moment
   On the shores of death and sin.

vi.

And the maiden she,
As conscious of a presence
Which she could not see,
Drew nearer round
A breast of snow
Her milk-white baldrich, bound
With roses in a row,
Which hung so loose and low
That the celestial light,
Heavenly and bright,
Shed from the soft wing's gleam,
Startled Irene Imogene.

vii.

One upward glance
And look askance

Startled Irene from her trance,
For in the heavens she saw
The god of virtue and of law,
Casting a covetous eye
On charms she would let die,
   'Neath the water's hem;
Hid from heaven
   And hid from men.

VIII.

She would have flown,
But for the tone
   And gesture mild
With which Ione
   Bespoke this queenly child.

IX.

"Art thou," he said,
"A heavenly form
   Or earthly maid?
For in these skies,
My very eyes
Are blinded with the light
Of Paradise
All fair and bright.
So that now
I may not say,

If thine be a mortal brow,
Or an angel's fair,
Who hath lost her way
In wandering through
The gates of heaven,
Which sometimes are
Left standing shut,
Or just ajar,
To admit angels of mercy,
Gone on missions wide,
To meet and guide
Earth's vanishing souls
Over the angry tide,
When death's bell tolls
Its softened chimes
On the celestial lakelet's side."

X.

While speaking there,
This god of air
Alighted on the bank
Of flowerets fair,
As Irene, in reply,
With beaming face
And sparkling eye,
Simply answered, "Mortal I."

XI.

A scene more bright
Never lit this land
Of death and night,
For Ione's pure heavenly light
Fell glorious round
That spot of earth
And flowery ground,
While the gates of paradise
Seemed opening wide,
To usher in
From death and sin
Ione and his queenly bride.

XII.

While apart they stood,
Heavenly they seemed, and good,
As angels bright of celestial sisterhood:
But when the divine
And mortal touch,
Mingled in love's embrace,
A shadow dimmed
The God-like face,
While rays from heaven's gate,
All darkly falling,
Too plainly told their fate.

XIII.

Their passion spent
In love's torment,
E'en the daisies where they lay
Seemed withering with the fires
Of the judgment day;
While from the charnel pit,
Shapes of hell did fly and flit,
Crippled, wild, untame,
Formless without name;
Amid the dance of death,
They poisoned e'en the very breath
This guilty pair
Breathed out of the air,
For flickering death lights
Glimmered and glistened there.

XIV.

The god with anger then
Cursed this daughter fair of men,
With oaths that must have come
From the death chant
His heavenly partners sung,
When the prince of darkness fell
From his high estate
Down to the gates of hell.

XV.

Irene's reply
Was equal wild and high,
Against the god
Who robbed her of the sky;
While the devil's moan
Dwindled to the very tone
Of fiendish mockery,
As her wailings of despair
Filled all the hideous air.

XVI.

Then I saw the tide
Bear a boatman pale
To the river's side,
And they went floating away
Over the waters wild and wide,
To the judgment day;
Each with their sin,
Stamped and moulded in
Their very souls,
Ever more to torment,
As the fires of duration spread
Round each guilty head,
Burning blue, burning red,
In the valley of Gehenna,
Roods beyond the realm of the dead.

THE PERI'S PARDON.

Amid the wind's low sighing,
Once a Peri earthward flying,
Saw a ruined maiden crying,
As if her heart was dying;
She sat amid the shrine
Of dark infamy and crime,
But the Peri, all divine,
Spoke to her in heavenly rhyme:

"Daughter of Eve so fair,
Why sit you sorrowing there?
There's mercy yet to spare,
From the God of earth and air,
For those who will but pray,
And sin's cursed minions put away.
Then be born again to-day,
And leave its dreadful way."

I would you had been there,
To hear the mingled prayer

Of the maid and angel rare,
Speeding to the gates of God so fair;
While they knelt them down
Amid ruins old and brown,
And a silence all profound
Fell on the consecrated ground.

A light too bright for mortal eye
Fell on them from the sky,
While through heaven went the cry:
"For such did Christ, the Savior, die."
The blest Peri's gone,
And the maiden walks among
The day's new dawn,
Filled with a heavenly song.

She holds a shepherd's wand
In her sinless hand,
Straying along the strand
Like being of another land;
In meek simplicity of grace,
With fair and radiant face,
Like one of the seraph race,
Grazing flocks from place to place.

THE FOUNTAIN OF YOUTH.

The golden morn is breaking;
The night of grief is past;
The charms of life are waking
By the wooing of the blast.

The merry lark is singing;
The brook is running clear;
The chapel bells are ringing
Out their sounds of cheer.

The farmer boy is whistling:
The maiden's face is fair;
The tender little nursling
Grows stronger in the balmy air.

The woods and meadows are aglow,
Tinged with a heavenly shine;
The rills go rippling with a flow,
Breathing music almost divine.

In truth, there seems to be
Some soft and holy spell,
Floating on the silvery sea,
From lands where angels dwell.

Brightening the face of day
And all nature's hue,
With an effulgent ray,
Both grand and new.

This land of Bula bright,
Embowered in a sunny dell,
Is the fount of youth's delight,
Where no decrepit mortals dwell.

'Tis just beyond the stream
Of darkly mirrored shades,
Where light's eternal gleam
In splendor breaks, o'er angelic maids.

We are nearing that strand,
With a silent, onward roll,
Where waiting friends do stand,
To welcome the immortal soul.

DEATH IN THE REAR.

I.

Once on a time,
A Christian, heavenly divine,
In a sunny clime,
Where the myrtle and the eglantine
Bloomed with fragrance rare,
Ran the race of care,
Over a rugged way,
Leading from earth
To the gates of day.

II.

As that Christian ran,
I saw a man,
Right in the van,
With lifted hand
And spear upraised,
And as I gazed,
Methought he threw
Darts at the Christian
As he flew.

III.

In wild disorder there,
With bosoms bare

And lifted hair,
Ran the running pair,
With all the speed
Of a warlike steed,
Rushing madly o'er
The ground, where thousands
Welter in their gore.

IV.

The face of Christian beamed
With light, like that which gleamed,
And flowing streamed,
In glorious grandeur teemed
Over the mount of God,
When Moses downward trod,
Bearing the tables of stone
To a wandering world
With sin o'erflown.

V.

The face of Death then,
Seemed horrid to the human ken,
Running o'er mount and glen,
In and out the files of men,
Pursuing that holy soul,
Fleeing to some goal,
Deep hidden from the eye,

Amid the mists and mystery
Of a silent, soundless sky.

VI.

Then methought there flew,
From Death's cold hand
A dart of shining hue,
Which found lodgment true
In the heart of him
Who ran from Death and sin;
At which Christian fell,
'Neath the cruel blow
And the victor's yell.

VII.

The fiend, 'twas plain to see,
Laughed in horrid glee,
Gloating o'er his victory,
As the Christian's blood ran free;
And he held his dance,
With strange expression of countenance,
All through the night forlorn,
Of Death's cold damps
Setting round the fallen form.

VIII.

But at the breaking day
When monks kneel down to pray,
The Christian rose from where he lay,

And went winging away
With a band of angels bright,
Beyond the distant range
Of Death's keen dart,
And ways of darkness strange.

IX.

And Death went then,
Searching for other men,
Over mountain, hill and glen,
With shaft upraised again;
And most faithful he
Kept up his archery,
Killing as he run
The stalwart man,
And widow's only son.

X.

From morn till rising sun,
Their dying cry rung
As earth's orb outward spun,
And into space swung;
But at times there came
Rays, brighter than flame,
From a fair celestial land,
Where Death shall nevermore
Raise his cold right hand,
To strike a mortal on that shore.

ELZA DREVE.

I.

One beautiful eve
Near the river Rhine,
I met my Elza Dreve,
'Neath the soft moonshine.

II.

The winds whispered love,
   And the rippling waters too
Reflected back the dove,
   Sporting with the wild cuckoo.

III.

Cupid's curious bow rang,
   As the speeding dart,
With gold and silver twang,
   Went thrilling through the heart.

IV.

And a love light then,
   With radiance softly fine,
Lit mountain, hill and glen,
   All 'round the river Rhine.

V.

I clasped the tender hand
   Of my lady fair,
Standing on the strand
   Of the rippling river there.

VI.

I looked into her eyes,
   And something in them seemed
Akin to spirits in the skies,
   That softly glowed and gleamed;

VII.

Like some immortal thing,
   A moment lingering there,
Shortly to take wing
   And mount the fields of air.

VIII.

I tried to see
   In that brief span
Her being's key,
   As the restless waters ran.

IX.

But the riddle strange
   Deep hidden lay,

Beyond my mental range,
   Where mortal might not stray.

X.

Then some mysterious spell,
   From out the clouds,
Over mount and valley fell,
   Like silken, sounding shrouds.

XI.

And in that soul eclipse,
   Love's mysterious thrill
Mingled at the touching lips,
   As night settled on wood and hill.

A HUT IN THE FOREST.

A little hut, that's all my own,
    Within a forest far,
Is built of wood and stone,
    Just under the northern star.

This little hut so rude
    And rough to see,
Once was tenanted by an angel good,
    Who was more than wife to me.

But a dark and dreary shade,
    Came through the open door,
And took my fairy maid
    To the far off, golden shore.

Before she went, she wove a spell
    Of some strange magic 'round,
So here alone I dwell
    In peace, with my faithful hound.

And naught doth our pleasure mar;
   This little home to me
Is brighter far than any star
   That shines on land or sea.

I found this bride of mine
   All fetterless and free,
In a fair, Italian clime.
   Oh! she was the world to me.

Some soft and heavenly sound,
   Seraphic and divine,
Comes floating 'round
   This home of mine.

And never base-tongued treachery,
   Hath broke the spell,
Which 'round my home so free,
   Doth on the breezes swell.

And now and then a note of love,
   Comes floating down the ether line,
From that angelic being above,
   To this rude hut of mine.

'Round this island in the sea,
   So far remote from sin,

Shines a golden beauty on every tree
   That hems my little cottage in.

And I'm waiting now that she
   May part the clouds of hope,
Which fell so thick o'er me
   When her thread of life broke.

And I know that heavenly one,
   When I am called to go,
Will greet me with a song—
   There's something tells me so.

THOSE CELESTIAL BELLS.

Throughout the heavenly dells,
There softly sinks and swells,
The rhyming and the chiming
Of fair celestial bells;
Blending with angelic mimes
Their symphonetic chimes,
And roll of golden notes,
Which through the ether calm floats.

In the land where the Jordan swells,
Some vague tradition tells
Of the welling and the knelling
Of bright celestial bells,
When some repentant one,
Weary wins the golden goal;
And a jeweled crown bedight
In lands of love and light.

There sparkling water wells,
At recurring intervals,
As the swinging and the ringing

Of those clestial bells
Wake the holy flow of soul,
With a silver-sounding roll,
Much like perennial showers
Shed on a paradise of flowers.

The glorious chorus tells
Of the joy that impels,
At the swaying and the swinging
Of those celestial bells;
Moving the silver leaves
On golden-shafted trees,
Whose verdant foliage rare
Shelter makes for angels fair;

Where blooming asphodels,
And blushing hairbells,
Move at the tinkling and the jingling
Of those celestial bells,
Borne on the balmy breeze,
Over silver-crested seas,
Whose bright refulgent beams,
Mingle with the light eternal's gleams.

There soft, sweet music swells,
Amid heavenly hills and dells,
All gently flowing and golden going,

From the celestial bells,
As sextons of eternity ring;
And angels their hosannas sing,
With an immortal strain
On the high and holy plain.

Oh, such hallowed spells,
As sometimes floats and swells,
Serenely and supremely
From those celestial bells,
Pouring sweet pæans of bliss,
On rivers of sacredness,
Where little cherubs bathe
In that love-creating wave.

Oh, let the angels sing!
And let the bliss of heaven ring,
To the rhyme and golden chime
Of those celestial bells;
Oh, let the music flowing
Through the soul be going!
For 'twill purer be
From that heavenly minstrelsy.

Oh, raise your cheering swells,
Through all the heavenly dells!
Let sweetest rhymes and softest chimes,

Flow out, celestial bells,
Over the far, wide sea,
Where sailing and floating free,
Goes Charon's ferry line
To the land of eternal sunshine.

THE CHIMNEY SWEEP.

Lonely and late,
Struggling with fate,
Went a chimney sweep by,
Under the dark, lowering sky;
Along poverty's bleak line,
Through the fast drifting snow
And the ebbing and flow
Of the tide of old time,
In the long, long ago.

The city lights shone
Like a silver-tipped throne
Through the dark, murky air,
With a false flashing glare;
And the grim visaged people
Seemed a burden to roll
On his lonely lone soul,
Like a groan from the steeple,
Rung out of eternity's goal.

Oh, the bitterest woes
The chimney sweep knows,

Are heaped upon him
When the night gathers in;
As he sinks down to rest
On the bleak, barren wold,
Half frozen with cold,
With a load on his breast,
Far away from the fold.

All deserted and lone,
What can he do but moan;
And his condition bewail,
As the merciless hail
Rattles down the dim sky,
Beating in wilderment wild,
On the chimney sweep child,
All forsaken to die
In the drifts deep piled.

Oh, strange it may seem!
Through his dying dream,
He saw a band of angels bright
Coming to him that night,
With a robe of glory fine,
As he went wandering away
Over the bleak, barren way,
From the fold of the ninety and nine,
To where the imps of misery stray.

THE CHIMNEY SWEEP.

And a sad refrain,
With softest strain,
Those messengers fair,
Sung over the dying there;
While a ray of gold,
In brilliant brightness shone
Down from Alla's throne,
On the chimney sweep cold,
At his last faltered moan.

Although the earth be drear,
There's sunshine in the upper sphere,
For the lonely and lone,
Who have no home;
Though friends may not be
Watching the soul's flight,
Through the last weary night,
Waiting stand a company,
Unseen to mortal sight.

Go aid the chimney sweep,
Up life's stubborn steep,
For he hath a whiter soul
Than many who stroll
In lordly garments by,
Honored with earth's renown,
And a golden crown,

Who never reach the sky
When their sun of life goes down.

Over there, perchance,
In the broad expanse
Of eternal pleasure,
Through hours of celestial leisure,
Crowned with a diadem,
Playing on a harp of gold,
Sheltered in the heavenly fold,
He'll greet us kindly
When the mists are backward rolled.

THE MISTS OF THE MORNING.

The rising mists of morning,
   Tell us daybreak is anear,
And soon the cloudy sky
   Will all be bright and clear.

The merry lark is caroling
   A softly tuneful lay,
And golden light is sparkling
   Around the fount of day.

All brightly glows and gleams,
   The bridge of celestial tapestry,
O'er which loving angels go,
   Bearing the holy dead away.

The shores of the better land,
   Break dimly on the view,
While waiting angels
   Are beckoning me and you.

The river of death
   Glides swiftly between,

But it hath no terrors
   In all that gilded scene.

For a heavenly step divine
   Hath the river spanned,
And God's eternal Son
   Reaches to us his own right hand.

Away beyond the river's brink,
   A celestial city stands,
Whose fair inhabitants
   Are bright angel bands.

Where the weary soul,
   May bathe in endless bliss,
In the eternal flow
   Of the river of sacredness.

DESPAIR.

Once on a time,
While I mourned
Over some mishap of mine,
The ghastly raven of despair
Came croaking 'round me there,
With such a hideous strain,
That I deemed
Some sea witch of the main
Had lent her aid
To torture and to pain
My half-crazed brain.

While thus I pondered,
    As in thought's deep maze,
I strayed and wandered
    Over dark and devious ways;
There came to me
A form divinely fair,
A radiant angel rare,
Straight from the fields of paradise,
Cheering my soul's despair.

In her soft, white hand
She bore a silver wand,
And wore a golden crown,
All sparkling bright
With jewels 'round,
Which dimmed my mortal sight.

With uplifted wand,
And countenance divine,
She gave command
Unto that croaking thing,
To "instantly take wing,
Nor dare to longer sing
That dismal dirge of thine
Beyond the dominions of thy king."

Then methought the croaking bird
Gave utterance to
The one lone word
"Despair," in such a wearied tone,
And ghastly, gurgled groan,
That I felt the marrow freezing
Slowly in my bone.

With eyes aflame,
And features much the same,
An elfin shape he took,

With all of Satan's look.
As 'round and 'round he flew,
His weird unearthly cries
Shook the vaulted skies,
And thrilled my being through.

Then 'round about me there,
The angel, with Despair,
Fought a battle in the air;
While dismal shafts of doom
Flew in arrowy keenness
From the vaulted tomb;
Till the angel's lance of hope,
Circling brightly then,
Told this enemy of men,
With it he could no longer cope.

'Twas plain to see,
   The angel's bearing bold,
Was an emanation of the Deity,
   And of no earthly mold;
That some power divine
Had shaped its heraldic shrine,
For it did gleam
With resplendent beam,
And plainly told to me
That this bird of misery,

This ominous thing,
Of dark and dreary wing,
Of which all the race have heard,
Croaking the one lone word,
In such a ghastly strain,
Even then I felt it burning
In my brain,
And the mind in its citadel turning
From all of human kind.

'Twas plain, I say,
That this melancholy fowl,
This ghastly, green-eyed ghoul,
This ancient thief of human prey,
Gloomy grown, and gray,
Fattening on the sighs,
Which for ages long
Have rent the skies,
Like the burden of a song,
From the many millions
Bearing their load of grief
Over the highway of life,
Longing for relief
From earth's care and strife.

Yes, 'twas plain to me,
That this croaking thing,

Of darkly sable wing,
From regions, none knoweth where,
Was no match at battling in the air;
For the radiant angel rare,
With her silvery lance
Cut right and left askance,
Till wounded in the strife,
The raven then
Sought refuge for his life,
Never looking 'round
Till those dim dominions
He had found,
Where the broodings of hate
Walk hand in hand with fate,
All dire and desolate;
In regions where never ray,
Lights up the darkling way.

When that croaking thing
Had taken wing
And flown away,
My spirits were so gay,
That I half believed
It made me better
For having grieved.

And ever since,
When the raven comes to me,
That bright angel I do see,
Chasing the ominous bird
To shores remote
Where he may gloat
With eternal glee,
And croak his dirge
Of sickening minstrelsy,
Through those dim dominions 'round,
Where never sound
Of cheerful note
Escapes a living throat
On those shores remote,
All dark and dreary,
As the midnight's sable wing,
Where lives no living thing.

THE STREAM OF TIME.

I.

A wonderful stream
Is the stream of time;
With its deeds of darkness
Of murder and crime;
Flowing through every land,
Through every clime,
With an onward sweep and swell,
To realms where fleshless mortals dwell.

II.

Beneath its turbulent wave
Hath perished many an immortal soul,
The Lord Omnipotent gave,
Fashioned for an eternal goal,
While struggling to get through
The breakers of life,
With the harbor full in view,
With flower and fragrance rife;
Where the merry song of birds
And the tuneful breezes swell,
Wake all the pulsations of life
That in human bosoms dwell.

III.

And oh, to go down in sight of this,
Were all of hell's deep wretchedness!
With only a shortened space
Between the perishing swimmer
And life's immortal landing place.

IV.

Yet many an one hath sunk
Beneath the waves of passion's sweep;
Who hath madly, darkly drunk
Life's poisoned chalice
Low and deep;
When the harbor bar
Broke round them glowing,
Like an illumined star
In the fields of ether far
With heavenly light o'erflowing.

V.

While only now and then
Some swimmer of immortal mould
Emerges from the water's hem
To tread those shores of gold,
Lying beyond our human ken
And the strand of eternity's wold.

VI.

Thus hath it always been,
And will be on forever,

With the mighty herds of men
Struggling in this restless river,
Amid breakers, shoals and sands,
And a polluted flow,
Ebbing from all earth's lands,
As to eternity we go;
Darkening black and drear
The waters that else might flow,
Eternal, bright and clear,
Past the beacon lights of cheer,
Which softly glow and gleam
Amid celestial atmosphere.

VII.

There's a light house on the strand,
And one on every hand,
To guide us past the shoals
With these immortal souls,
As the river onward rolls;
And the glorious keepers, too,
Of fair, celestial hue,
Waft the lamp of life
To me and you,
From inlet, creek and haven too.
Where all may shelter gain
From the river's turbulent main,
On the glorious, golden shore,

Never stained by human gore;
Fair as the fountain of day,
Where silvered rills of bliss,
Murmuring, meander away,
Through groves of shadiness.

VIII.

Oh, the resistless sweep
Of the river broad and deep
Hath borne away our brightest joys,
Like worthless baby toys;
Hath buried hope's bright queen
Beneath the shade and sheen
Of its fathomless roll
Before the eye of the frenzied soul;
Poised for eternal flight
From the outmost plank of time,
On wings of heavenly shine.

IX.

A wonderful stream
Is the stream of time,
With its deeds of darkness
Of murder and crime;
Flowing through every land,
Through every clime,
With an onward sweep and swell,
To realms where fleshless mortals dwell.

THE IMMORTAL MASTERS.

Once they lived
   For life and fame,
Dying they were buried
   On the world's wide domain;
But now their sphere,
   Ah, who may name!

In the forum, in the furrow,
   In the senate, at the loom;
One by one they passed away,
   Plodding onward to the tomb.

In the pulpit, on the bench,
   In poverty's cheerless gloom;
One by one they passed away,
   Plodding onward to the tomb.

On the throne and at the stake,
   Surrounded by life's sweet bloom;
One by one they passed away,
   Plodding onward to the tomb.

Some in the strife of battle's broil,
   And some we thought too soon;
One by one they passed away,
   Plodding onward to the tomb.

Some on the ocean's watery waste,
   Some 'neath the wild festoon;
One by one they passed away,
   Plodding onward to the tomb.

Some at the polar line,
   Some by the bursting bomb;
One by one they passed away,
   Plodding onward to the tomb.

Some in Afric's jungles dread,
   Some in the cloud-capped balloon;
One by one they passed away,
   Plodding onward to the tomb.

Some fell in manhood's morn,
   Some at its eve, others at its noon;
One by one they passed away,
   Plodding onward to the tomb.

Some lines remain to tell,
   Some sculptured urns their doom;

One by one they passed away.
   Plodding onward to the tomb.

Shall we ever meet them more,
   As the eternal ages speed away,
Where life, beauty and bloom
   Pass forever onward, from the tomb.

THE HARP OF A HAND THAT'S STILL.

That harp of gold,
   I love it much;
'Twas moved of old
   By a heavenly touch.

A wanderer of the air,
   With look of love,
And form divinely fair,
   Came from the courts above.

And in the golden eventide,
   Like a thrill of life divine,
Would waft sweet music wide,
   From that harp of mine.

Over its shining keys
   Would moving fingers stray;
More beautiful than these
   Made of earthly clay.

Over its well-tuned strings,
   And sounding bridge of song,

Would move celestial warblings,
   In the twilight's dusky dawn.

In that holy spell,
   A slender ring of flame
Shone round the harp I loved so well,
   And the heavenly player's name.

She was mortal once on earth,
   And sweetheart true to me;
But angels coveted her birth
   And took her beyond the crystal sea.

She left the harp behind,
   As a fond memento dear;
To cheer my drooping mind
   While waiting the dawning near.

And when I lonely seem,
   And longing to be there,
Will come my angel queen
   And sing to my soul's despair

Such sweet harmonious strains,
   That passion's stormy roll
No longer frets and pains
   My weary, half-sick soul.

THE HARP OF A HAND THAT'S STILL.

Oh, do not strike that harp
   With rude or vulgar hand;
For 'twould break my heart
   And pain her of the angel band.

But let it ever stay
   Unmoved by human touch,
Where she may come and play—
   For I love its music much.

It thrills my being through,
   Like the glance of an angel's eye,
With bright celestial hue,
   Cast on sinners from the sky.

You may this feeble lay deplore;
   But to me that harp of gold
Is more than earthly store,
   Or shepherd's finest fold.

Her dear and gentle hand
   Played divinely gifted lays,
As we wended on the strand,
   In those early, sunny days.

Yes, I love that harp of old,
   And more precious to me

Than rubies fine, or rarest gold,
   Is each bright and shining key.

I keep it yet, and always will,
   And fain would I keep it nice;
In memory of my angel still
   Who walks the fields of paradise.

CELESTIAL MELODIES OF THE AIR.

There's music in the air,
Softly floating everywhere
Round about the golden stair,
Leading to a scene so very fair;
And we sometimes catch a note
As it round about doth float
From the land so far remote,
Like the bulbul's softest tune,
Poured to the silvery moon
On some evening fair in June.

Those singers celestial sing,
Poised on viewless wing,
Through winter and through spring,
And round about us fling
Hope's bright, golden maze,
On dark and lowering days,
As time onward strays,
To a harbor near at hand,
Where sing the singing band
Beckoning us to its strand.

In the golden summer time
There seems to float and chime
A sweet celestial rhyme
Adown the ether line;
Which thrills us like a spell
Through the woof of magic woven well,
In and out some sunny dell
Where fays and fairies dwell;
Waking a holy flow of soul
At the celestial music's roll.

Sometimes there sinks and swells
The chiming of soft, celestial bells,
Which cast those holy spells
From realms where God eternal dwells;
But we may not know
The full sweetness of the flow
While lingering here below,
As the sunbeams onward go;
For that seraphic monotone
Comes from a shore unknown.

And as I've sometimes read
Books of the living and the dead,
Would come a saintly tread
Flitting round my head,
With a harp celestial, bright,

In heavenly robes bedight,
Making music light
Move the fount of love's delight;
When life's discords would chill
Me wandering down its hill.

I've floated on the river Nile
Far from human guile,
In rapt, deep thought the while,
Seeking some sinless isle.
Oh, then it sweetly blended
Where life and strife were ended,
In that realm from sin defended,
As my boat onward wended,
In the softest, sweetest strain,
That ever thrilled the human brain.

And as this isle I neared,
To the imagination there appeared
Forms all white and weird,
Which man hath feared;
Singing on the strand
With a heavenly sister band,
Under Tan Sein's command,
With silvered harp and wand,
Angel's songs which seem
The lingering traces of a dream.

There I waited round
That enchanted island ground,
Listening to the heavenly sound,
Till the full, bright moon went down;
And the latest line
Of that song divine,
Rings in these ears of mine,
As when I left that sunny clime
And went wandering through other lands,
Searching for fairer strands.

LOVE AND TIME.

Love and Time go speeding on
   Through many a sunny clime,
But they do not journey long
   Ere they meet the day's decline.

They haste o'er fragrant meads
   Where flowers in beauty bloom,
To a way that winding leads
   Onward to the tomb.

Through the golden morning light,
   They glide with laughter by;
Heedless of the coming night
   Setting round them in the sky.

Hope's bright, celestial ray
   Breaks on their vision now,
And angel forms about them play
   With jeweled crowns upon their brow.

Amid the dawn of Love's delight
   They see a splendid palace near;

Dazzling to the mortal sight,
   And filled with friendly cheer.

They think that castle grand is theirs,
   Built by the lord of Love's own isle;
With golden glowing stairs
   And a bright bower beyond the stile.

But as they near the mansion fair
   To them it shadowy seems,
Like those forms of air
   We sometimes see in dreams.

And when they through the postern stray
   A mountain hard to climb,
All round with copsewood gray,
   Dims the landscape's shine.

Then Love leaves Time behind
   And speeds throughout the air,
To a shore man may never find,
   Bright, beautiful and fair.

Love ran on in such a hurry,
   That Time was doomed to wait
A little space and worry,
   Complaining of his fate.

Through all the distant round
    Of days and nights so long,
This angel again he never found
    To cheer him with her song.

No mortal made by the hand above,
    Upon this shoal of time,
Can keep pace with the god of love
    Where the hill of life's to climb.

THE POET'S DEPARTED SHADES.

The poet's departed shades,
When evening's twilight fades,
Sometimes waft us here
Light from the celestial atmosphere,
Filling the homes and haunts of men
With their silent muse again.

At such recurring times,
When the harp of nature chimes,
Come glimpses of a better land
And a more friendly strand,
Brightly streaming o'er
The rolling waters drear
From the poets' words of cheer.

Those gifted bards sublime
Have left their foot prints
"On the sands of time,"
That some discouraged swain,
Soul-sick and drooping
May take heart again,
And bravely buffeting life's ills

Upon its angry main;
Part the water's spray
With more than mortal vigil,
And gain the gates of day
Beyond the harbor eternal,
Where beacon lights supernal
Gleam with a golden ray
All bright and clear,
Through the soft, celestial atmosphere.

THE SHADOWS OF THE NIGHT.

When the shadows of the night
    Come floating 'round my open door,
I ofttimes think of the departed,
    Those who have gone to the other shore.

Then the sound of rustling robes
    Falls gently on my ear;
And light comes streaming through the darkness,
    Down from the celestial atmosphere.

And those I loved so dearly
    Come flitting through the gloom,
To trim the burning taper
    Dimly burning at the tomb.

Then the voices of the night
    Mingle with the flow of time,
In a sort of solemn cadence,
    Like the ghastly mariner's rhyme.

And the whisperings of Death
    Create a feverish chill,

Rising from the meadow
  Over the woodland and the hill.

Then I seem to catch the sound
  Of some silvery chiming bell,
Floating through the darkness
  From lands where fleshless mortals dwell.

And I hear the dashing wave
  Break on the nearing strand;
As I wander onward
  To the fair, appointed land.

In my imagination, then,
  I hear the grating keel
Of Charon's boat, as he helps on board
  His human cargo, with hand of steel.

DARTS OF DEATH.

Darts of death are flying
   Thickly all around,
And everywhere men are trying
   To escape the fatal wound.

But the heartless archer
   Pulls at the gilded bow,
And the shining arrows' whirr
   Maketh the life stream flow.

This shade of grisly shapes
   Hath stained life's pages
With the blood he daily takes,
   For lo! these many ages.

He roams about in glee,
   Marring the form divine
With his cruel archery,
   Through every land and clime.

His shining shafts are hurled
   With a determined will,

DARTS OF DEATH.

And nowhere in the world
   Can one avoid his will.

The fair and gentle form
   He often takes away;
Leaving the decrepit and forlorn
   For his coming another day.

His step is firm and true,
   His hand is cold and lean;
His bow is of gilded hue;
   And he walks with dreadful mein.

And mourners follow when
   He takes from earth away
Its true and manly men,
   Like a stolen robber's prey.

Oh, that this fearful shade
   And phantom of our homes
Would quit his dread parade,
   And stop these earthly groans!

Then, methinks would be
   The dawning day of bliss;
When no darts would flee
   To change earth's happiness.

Without this dreaded shape,
    We might live in endless dawn;
And a beautiful kingdom make
    Filled with eternal song.

But our brief span,
    Too short it is,
While on this earthly strand,
    To attain to this.

Where such an archer bold
    Culls in daily round
Immortal fatlings from the fold,
    Like a tiger's dread rebound.

No breastplate can shield
    From the darts of death;
While in life's fruitful field
    Time with sickle wandereth.

But happy perchance if we,
    In the long hereafter, may
Avoid this villain's archery,
    Beyond the darkling river's spray.

Where no death or mildew blights
    The immortal work of God,

Through age's celestial delights,
  On shores where archer never trod.

Oh, then, we may build
  A city fair to see,
With all earth's millions filled,
  Through the long eternity.

A POET OF A GOLDEN AGE.

A poet of a golden age,
With a wreath of glory round him,
Went journeying on pilgrimage
With a vision all unbounden;
Through Afric's sunny land,
Through sultry Hindoostan,
Through merry England,
He roamed about in glee,
The wonders of the world to see.

He went to ancient Rome,
Straight from St. Peter's dome,
All on the modern line,
Journeying thence to Palestine;
He had seen the Saviour's tomb
And heard the fig tree's doom,
And trod upon the strand
Of ancient Pharaoh's land,
And journeyed to the Nile
To see its maidens smile.

He had crossed the ocean free
And seen the land of liberty;
He had sailed around the pole,
And a glimpse of Satan stole,
When he led the Lord about,
And the lights of heaven went out
As he sought to barter away
The kingdoms of this world
For the gates of day,
Upon that mountain gray;
He had traversed earth and air,
Seen all that's grand and glorious there;
For 'twas his desire to be
A kind of earthly deity.

The poet was wise,
As you may surmise.
He'd looked into laughing eyes,
And sipped the nectar balm
Of love's delicious bliss,
And felt the cold qualm
Of a heart amiss.
He knew the wily train
Of arts to employ
Which captivate the female brain
With love's promised joy;
And ofttimes he found,

As he went journeying round,
Some gentle maiden fair
Who had for him a care.
But he only played
With her passion's swell,
For 'twas his delight
In love's bower to dwell,
Sporting in the ray
Of fairy fancy
Shed around his stay.

He knew all the charms
And false alarms
Of the female mind;
And his horn would wind
In softest tune to the balmy breeze,
Making music to the reapers,
Reaping on the leas.

He could talk in prose and rhyme,
And paint an image all divine.
He could see across the sea
Of dark mortality
Up to the gates of gold,
Where sing in ecstacy
The angel fold.

He could look far by
The throne of God on high,
And there decry
The mists of eternity
Floating in the sky.

There was no copulet
In prose or rhyme
Which he didn't learn,
And its meaning full discern;
Nor a mystery long concealed
Which to the amulet of his mind
Didn't stand revealed.

There wasn't a track
Or prudish quack,
Or hound of any pack,
But that he could avoid,
With his light and knowledge
Properly employed.

He could sound a shepherd's horn
All in the early morn,
Or tune a lady's reed,
Or ride a warlike steed
Over roughest mead.

He could guide a boat
Like a swan afloat,
Or spread a sail
To any gail
That ever blew
Through mist or hail.

And all his rhymes
Were like heavenly mimes,
Mingling with creation's chimes;
So tender, sweet,
So faultless, fair and neat,
Written to any measure
Or any feet.

He left no heir;
But many a maiden fair
Went wildly wandering
Through the gloom of dark despair,
On her condition pondering.

His name was Militage,
And he lived in a golden age,
When our earth was young,
And daily visited
By wanderers from the sun;
And blest Pirio fair,

From worlds of upper air;
By angels dear,
With wings all bright and clear,
Like radiant lights
Amid celestial atmosphere.

And when he did die
There was no pomp or burial;
They took him to the sky
In a shroud imperial;
But long since then
His shade hath strayed and walked with men,
Casting a fair, bright light
Through every darkened glen;
As if heralding the day
When all earth shall heavenward stray,
In that great call of time
When deeds shall be enacted
Eternal and sublime.

THE SEA OF GALILEE.

Once on the sea of Galilee
   There walked and trod
A personification of the Deity—
   The true and living God.

The winds were raging high,
   The waves did leap and roll,
Darkly dangerous was the sky,
   And angry all nature's soul.

A fisherman's band,
   In a vessel small,
Had left the strand
   And met the rising squall.

As the heaven-born heir
   Did on the waters walk,
The fishermen in despair
   With mystic speech began to talk.

"Some spirit of the deep
   Hath risen from its grave,

With foul and hideous sweep
　　To cast us in the wave.

"Ye elements lend your aid,
　　With strong and steady swell,
To shield us from the shade
　　Of misery's deepest hell."

"Be ye of good cheer,"
　　The holy Saviour said;
"'Tis I that's walking here:
　　Oh, be ye not afraid."

The winds were hushed,
　　The boisterous sea was stilled;
The fishermen in rapture gushed,
　　With heavenly happiness filled.

They reached the land,
　　And none was then afraid;
The Saviour with that fishing band
　　To the God of heaven prayed.

Thus, on the sea of Galilee
　　The feet of Jesus trod,
And led the fishermen free
　　To the harbor and to God.

WE COME AND GO.

We come and go,
Like the daisies and the snow,
   Mid silence all profound,
   In one eternal round,
Here below.

We come and go,
On high tide and low,
   Mid hopes and fears,
   Mid the flood of years,
Thus and so.

We come and go,
To reap and sow,
   Mid sunshine and rain,
   Mid pleasure, gift and pain,
As the wild winds blow.

We come and go,
Both friend and foe,
   Whom death calls away,
   Impatient of our stay
Here below.

We come and go,
Like the ebb and flow
  Of the tide of time,
  Bearing to a distant clime
All our happiness and woe.

We come and go,
'Neath the cloud and bow,
  Filled with suspense,
  As from whence to thence
We may not know.

We come and go,
In a ceaseless flow,
  To where the rust and mold
  Wears away the coffin lid of gold,
Slow, very slow.

We come and go,
The lofty and the low,
  Along a hidden line
  Of strange mystery divine,
In one unbroken flow.

We come and go,
Like the rainbow,
  Within the little space
  Alloted to our race
Here below.

We come and go,
Catching glimpses of a glow,
　As the eternal sheen
　Breaks with brightening beam,
When life's sun is getting low.

We come and go,
Each with his sorrow, O!
　The bondman and the free,
　Amid the deepest mystery,
Thus and so.

We come and go
To shades of death and woe,
　After a little stay,
　When the morn is getting gray,
And the clouds hang very low.

We come and go,
To the judgment, O!
　For sentence just,
　With the blest or curst,
Eternity will show.

We come and go
To where no snow
　Falls on those plains of light,
　Which Charon's boat so white
Hath touched for ages, O!

We come and go,
Surging to and fro
　With the restless throng,
　Singing poverty's song,
In the work-house here below.

We come and go,
The aged bending low
　At the brink of the grave,
　Affrighted by the wave,
All billowy bounding, O!

We come and go,
Both fast and slow,
　To heaven above,
　Where all is love,
From a world of sorrow.

We come and go,
Where no grasses grow,
　To regions dim,
　There to float and swim,
Through fire below.

We come and go,
While rivers overflow,
　Sailing far and wide
　On a shoreless tide,
To bliss or woe.

We come and go,
Ah well you know,
   To a mart of fear,
   All dismal, dark and drear,
Created long ago.

We come and go
Like the thrush and roe
   In the early spring,
   When the mavis sing,
And the earth's aglow.

We come and go
Like the crystal snow,
   Without a stain,
   Or thought of pain,
In the age eternal's flow.

We come and go
To sepulchers of woe,
   All stained in crime,
   With no messenger divine,
To point us heavenward, O!

We come and go,
Like the daisies and the snow,
   Mid silence all profound,
   In one eternal round,
Here below.

THE HEADLESS HORSEMAN.

I.

In a valley of the Hudson,
Some vague tradition,
Some chronicle of eld,
Is rife with legendary lore;
With quaint and curious superstitions,
With weird and wondrous musings,
Concerning a headless horseman
Which is nightly seen to go,
In strange, meteoric haste,
Cantering up and down
The meads and meadows there,
Pursuing some fleeting shadow
Which ever speeds before,
Alluring this wondrous horseman
Through the mists of the nether wold.

II.

'Tis said by ancient housewives,
And good old sires of the Dutcher line,

Whose ambition is to till
Those sunny nooks and vales
With the hand of frugal toil,
That this curious horseman
Fought in the Revolutionary wars
'Gainst the red coat Britishers,
Whose cannonading laid waste
The blooming vale,
With desolation and blood;
That he fought on Rouen's heights,
Shut off from the valiant free
By four and forty Britishers,
'Gainst dire and deadly odds;
That his silvery sword
Laid many a valiant low,
And of all that fought him there,
One alone survived
The terrible field of slaughter,
Whose well-directed cutlass
Severed from shoulders of manly mold,
The head that well had graced a king.

III.

But this horseman didn't die.
Changed by some mystic spell,
He led our fainting troops

Onward to victory's mead,
Where the golden sunlight
Of liberty's resplendent dawn
Drove the blinded Britishers
From freedom's holy shrine.

IV.

And now he nightly goes
From the silent churchyard
In quest of a missing head,
Led on by the sprite of the Britisher
Who did that hellish deed,
In the days long gone by,
When our immortal masters fought
For the land of liberty.

V.

The speed at which he rides
On recurring times
Is caused by being belated
In a fruitless search;
And he hies him hence,
To the church-yard still,
Ere the morning light
Reveals his shapeless form
To the rustic, woodland swain,

Ever plodding on awearily
In round of daily toil.

VI.

When out on such a mission,
His favorite trysting place
Is 'neath the branching tree
Under which the unfortunate
Major Andre was captured
And doomed to death
By the Continental array,
For being a spy from the British line.

VII.

In short, this sleepy valley,
For many miles around
Is rife with floating fancies
Concerning the spectre horseman.
And ill betide the hardy swain,
Who plodding homeward late,
In the peaceful Sabbath tide,
Meets this curious phantom
On his nightly rounds.
Fright and frenzy then
Chills the current of his soul,
Which the finer fancy

Of some loved Helena
Wakened with her magic touch.

VIII.

The stories that are told
Of this spectre shade,
Of his quirks and pranks
Around that valley fair,
Mounted like mortal trooper
On his wondrous steed
So white and clean,
With flowing mane of gold
And hoofs of silvered hue,
Would fill endless books,
And keep the angel of the sky
Writing historic tales
For ages yet to come.

IX.

Whatever the horseman is,
Whatever his name may be,
The superstition vague
Increases with the suns,
In that valley of the Hudson,
Where ghostly skulls
And crumbling bones

Fell striking for our flag;
And this headless horseman,
By some fatality strange,
Still courses through the valley
With matchless speed,
As if a curse lay on his soul,
Still urging him to find
The missing appendage;
That in the cavalcade to come
He may ride with leaders brave,
Along the banks of the Jordan fair,
On celestial review,
In the paradise above.

ANELBE AND THE ANGEL.

I.

One fair, bright eventide,
As the setting sun was shining,
I saw a maiden rare
On the velvet sward reclining;
Beside a crystal spring
Where float the swan and pelican
So light and free of wing;
Amid the silvered sheen
Of the water's silent gleam,
Which for ages long
Hath cleansed the pilgrim whole,
Doing penance for the immortal soul.

II.

Close beside her stood
One of the heavenly brotherhood,
Who had wandered from the way,
From the gates of gold,
From the celestial fold
And verge of eternal day;
Earthward on some mission sent

From heaven's high battlement,
By just Alla's care,
In search of a sinful tear
For joy's bright banquet in the air,
All penitent and clear.

III.

While winging too near the shade
The angel saw the maid,
Whose curls of fairest hue,
As he caught a nearer view,
Love's libation from the angel drew.

IV.

Ah, then, her splendid form
    And bewitching face
Awoke the passion's storm —
    And the angel fell from grace,
As many mortals fall,
Loosing God and heaven and all.

V.

Pausing one moment to drink
    Of the crystal tide,
Just to rest and think
    And linger at her side.
What frenzy of soul

Ran through his being whole,
As one kiss he stole,
And touched her mortal face
In love's embrace;
And the maiden fair
Of form and heavenly hue
Fond of the etherial wanderer grew.

VI.

For hours they lingered there
Without a thought or care
Of the future anywhere;
The moments seemed to go,
Like the heavenly thrill
None but angels know
On the delectable hill.

VII.

The love begun all harmless,
Ere they were aware
Went for amiss,
As Cupid sported 'round them there.

VIII.

The thrill of passion's pleasure past,
They woke from love's embrace at last,
To see guilt's dark disgrace

In every bower and place.
The angel gloomy grew,
Thinking of his fall;
And the sin of the maiden, too,
Was wormwood gall.

IX.

The maiden wicked changed,
As her soul down hell's pathway ranged,
Through tangled fern and darkest mead,
Pausing at no crime or deed.

X.

And when the offspring came
It took not mortal name,
No human shape or form;
Like child of sin and storm,
'Twas wayward, wicked, wild,
With body all defiled,
As if the blight of God
Had smitten with his avenging rod.

XI.

The angel sought some shade
Mid the depths of Afric's sandy sea,
Where never mortal maid
Again he might see;

Thinking to atone
With grief and groan
For his awful crime
By penitence sublime;
And on some distant day
Regain what Anelbe took away,
And be admitted free
Into the presence of the Deity.

XII.

The maiden, sin defiled and stained,
The throne of God profaned,
And step by step went down,
Till hell's deep center she had found;
In falsehood, crime and sin,
Her woman's soul plunged in,
Knew no bound or end;
Deserted, dying, without a friend,
Forsaken by her sect,
And e'en the holy angels
Did her death bed neglect.

XIII.

The offspring—none ever knew
What the King of Terror's put him to,
For he did excel in wickedness
The acts and deeds of hell;

But 'twas sometimes thought
He stirred the purgatorial pot,
As a compromise of his lot;
For he scarce lived to be
The stature of a man in majority
Ere some infernal shade
Spirited him away, by the aid
Of malignant souls,
To shores where eternity rolls.

XIV.

Oh, maidens fair,
And angels bright of air,
Avoid each other with a care!
Till the mystic change
Adown the grooves of time doth range,
And you are fitted fair
For celestial friendships
Of the air;
Guarded by the sinless sheen
Of Alla's light supreme
From over draughts of bliss
And distant flights of wickedness,
As the holy thrill of purity's soul
Runs on through the ages
In eternity's goal.

SIR ROBERT GIVES HAD SEVEN WIVES.

Sir Robert Gives had seven wives,
And they were much like bees in hives.
One ruling spirit there supreme
Asserted herself a royal queen;
With dark black eyes
That flashed like lightning in the skies,
And stern and haughty tread,
She held his household all in dread,
Casting consternation 'round,
At her footfall's angry sound.
Her flowing robes of gold
Rustled like wolf among the fold;
Her jeweled hand held high command;
And her sceptered brow
No familiarity would allow;
Cold, lofty and high,
She moved people somehow
By the flash of her eye.

Her name was Jabelle,
And she reigned so haughtily,
That even Sir Robert Gives,

Ah, yes, even he!
Dreaded to meet her with his eyes;
And 'twas like a death of doom
To pass an hour in the room,
When she summoned him
In the twilight's dusky dim,
To vent her venomous spleen,
With a vicious woman's vim
Or a daring devil's mien.

The next in line
Had a countenance divine,
And her name was Evangeline.
The apostle's creed
In the golden eventide she'd read,
For the peace of her soul,
As light 'round the pole,
Slowly vanished away
Like the mists of a spray,
Which so solemnly roll,
At the close of a Sabbath's day.

She could repeat the various creeds,
And would count her beads,
Like a monk with solemn face
In his chancel of grace;
And in Latin she'd tell

Of the angels in heaven
And the demons in hell.
In sorrow she'd moan
And mutter "Ave Mary" alone.
Holy incense she'd burn,
And 'round and 'round would turn,
Crossing herself in fear,
Fancying she could hear,
From a shadow standing near,
The doom of eternity spoken clear.

Sometimes a light supreme
Seemed breaking o'er her wildered dream,
Shining from the eternal strand
Along the borders of this earthly land.
She would ofttimes at night
Till broad daylight,
Full in Sir Robert's sight,
Go through her drill,
And all his passion kill.

"Alas," sighed he,
"She's no wife to me!
I cannot embrace her witchery,
Nor love such aerial thing,
Flying on mystic wing
In the May-time of the spring

Through those regions of dread
Leagues beyond the valley of the dead.

"Evangeline is too divine
For these arms of mine,
I'll seek a more material form.
What though she be shelterless,
Stained by earth's storm,
If she have love for me,
I'll greet her as some angel form,
Come to bear me company
Away from earth and night,
Into the beams of the paradise light,
Beyond the gates of gold,
Whose pearly portals fold
In silence there on angels rare
That never shall grow old."

Sir Robert's wife Minert
Was a regular feminine flirt,
The grandest at the ball
And the gayest in the hall.
She wore her ribbons and lace
With a kind of witching grace,
Smiling sweetly on the men,
Slyly winking now and then,
With a kind of killing air

Shooting Cupid's glances everywhere
With coquettish skill and care.
Living in an ideal world
With pleasure's pinions unfurled,
She tries each wily scheme
To make things not what they seem,
Just to fool some fashioned fop
By the dazzling light of her gleam.

Simple, soothing and light,
She wears rings and rubies bright,
Diamonds, pinks and pearls,
With a head of sunny curls,
Singing now and then a glee
To the fashion fops of frivolity;
Flirting with this one and that,
According to the color of his cravat;
Like the waters of the seas,
Always ill at ease,
While there's a rippling breeze;
Liking each new thing best,
Skipping and waltzing about
With alternate smile and pout,
Till nature's worn out.

"Alas," said Sir Robert Gives,
"That this egregious thing

Should be one of my wives.
She has smiles for other men,
Ned, Tim, Joe or Ben,
It matters not to her
Who may be her foppish worshiper,
For me her heart doth never stir;
It's much like an icicle's core,
On the creg or on the moor.
She's no wife to me
But a thing of gayety,
Sporting like the bee,
With any gaudy thing
That wafts a tinseled wing
Through the May-time of the spring."

The next was named Luellalorn,
With look of melancholy born.
All day she'd sit and sing
By a silver-crested spring,
Some sad and tender lay
To who'd thitherward stray,
As if she'd sing her life away.
Her face was very fair,
And almost hid
In ringlets of wavy hair.
Her brow was mild
As that of holy child

Sitting amid the shrine
Of some chaplet all divine.

Her speech was bland,
With mystic meaning
None could understand;
And a lonely look,
Like an open book,
Show'd she lived apart
From the common herd of men,
With some sorrow at her heart
Veiled from human ken,
Ever gnawing at her life,
E'en though she was Sir Robert's wife.

"Alas," thought he,
"She's living not for me,
But for some saint or deity.
What may I then
But mingle with men,
For her heart is cold,
And her robes of gold
Seem to enfold
Some fleshless mould,
Where no passions may
Move the fount of love's supernal play.

"Oh, I cannot love
Such a heartless dove,
Though her feathers fine
Be tipped with eternal sunshine;
I must break away
From this cruel fate to-day,
And find one of the earthly line
To soothe this soul of mine."

The next was Laomedrone,
A very odd crone,
Who was getting old;
And such a scold
None ever knew,
Save him she was wedded to.
She scolded at this and that—
If the meat was too fat,
Or if 'twas too lean,
Or when the grass was getting green,
Or because Victoria's queen.
If there was a mouse
About the house,
Or a cat to kill,
Her tongue would run on still
Like earth's great grinding mill.

She'd scold at the men
Till half-past ten;
She'd scold at the boys
For having toys;
She'd scold at the girls
For wearing curls;
She'd scold at the maid
For using yeast;
And she'd make the clergy afraid,
As well as the priest;
She fussed in the pew,
And kept the church in a stew,
The deacons in line
Would lose their grace divine
When she cast upon them her look benign.
In short, she was a jade,
And made Sir Robert afraid.

There was gloom within
   And gloom without,
And a mighty din
   When she let her tongue run out.

Sir Robert then
Bethought himself
The most accurst of men.
He couldn't speak,

He didn't try,
But up would leap
To meet that fiendish eye,
Only to be quelled,
Like those of eld,
By the magician's art
Strangely thrilling through the heart.

"Alas," thought he,
"What did I see
In that female fiend,
While in love's bower I dreamed
That witching dream,
That I could wed
And take her to my bed!
There must have been
Some mischief in my head."

The next was Lady Gale,
A regular tell-tale.
She knew the ups and downs
Of all the lanes and rounds;
And could follow a track
Like a trained pack
Of Saint Hubert's hounds.
She would rather meet
A neighbor in the street

And spin a yarn,
Than knit socks of yarn.

She knew the news,
And the kind of shoes
Each living mortal wore
For many miles around her door;
She knew the styles
And beau-catching smiles
That Mrs. Pink and Purdy wore;
For once she saw a man
With a lady's fan
Come out of the back room door.

She knew Mr. Pert and Prandle,
And when once a breeze of scandle
Rose, she knew full well
The art to make it swell
And keep the thing agoing,
For she was very knowing.
In short she was versed
In all the accurst
Rumors that will float
Round a village remote,
Where the women and the men,
Talk and talk back again,
For want of better work to do;

Lounging the lazy season through,
As the sunbeams onward go
With bright, refulgent flow,
Gilding the hills of God
With gold and amber rod,
Like some angelic spell
Thrown round Sailen's citadel.

"Alas," Sir Robert thought,
"Mine is a lively lot,
  Living in this Eden fair,
  'Neath the glance of a devil's stare;
For what may happiness be
When you pluck marital fruit
From a gnarled and twisted tree.

"I'll put her away,
  For she'd make trouble for God
On the judgment day,
  With her tongue and her nod;
And should the devil get her,
There'll be a stir
In his majesty's domain
When her tongue's let loose again,
After that distant sweep
Across the river deep,
Where parting is no pain."

The last in line
Was named Avergevine,
And to jealousy did incline.
If Sir Robert tipped his hat
To girl or brat,
She thought there was
Something strange in that;
She would sit and cry
If the glance of his eye
Fell round the room,
Or a cheek of bloom
Changed color because
She herself broke etiquette's laws,
In gazing to see
If that hasty glance,
By any mischance,
Moved the fount of female witchery.

'Twas the same in Rome
And the same at home,
Whether in a crowd
Or left alone;
Her jealous heart
Trains of thought would start
When the braggart's vim
Brought a smile from him,
Or the strangest story told,

Caused Sir Robert to laugh
And his sides to hold,
Till the shining gold
Would shimmer and gleam,
Like shadow's sheen,
Softly flitting by,
Borne on Peri's wings
Athwart the sky;
For the deep well of laughter
Is located on high,
And in that bright realm
It never runs dry.

"Strange," said he,
"There is no peace for me
In all this lady line;
Not one there is
Who is wife of mine.
That sacred name
Wakes a kindred flame,
Which always should burn on
Like daylight after dawn.

"But the cold eclipse
Of a woman's lips
Chills the flow
Of the passion's swell,

Like darts of death
Thrown at love's citadel.

"Oh, the willful frown
  Of a thing that wears a gown
  Will chase from me
  The last bright smile of courtesy;
  And all the golden hue,
  Without love's return,
  Can wake no sympathy
  Where it is due;
  This much I discern."

Gentle friend,
Wherever you wend,
There is a line
I'd have you learn
From the dial plate of time,
As 'round and 'round we run:
No wife can be
True wife to you or me
Where there's no heaven-born sympathy;
But where a mutual flow
Of true friendship,
From two souls doth go
At the touching of the lip,

There spirits meet and sip
The nectar dew
From love's golden chalice
Deeply dipped in the fount of eternal hue.

They may pass away
From out this mortal strife,
But beyond the resurrection day
The true born man and wife
Will meet to love,
For love is life,
And God is love.

MILDRED.

By the ancients it is told
How the love god Eros walked and strolled
   Along the river Nile,
Entranced with the witchery
   Of the maiden Mildred's heavenly smile.

'Twas in the autumn's golden prime,
When the evening bells were ringing out their chime,
   And light from the lamps of heaven all
Resplendent on their pathway
   Did float and fall.

When an angel band bedight,
With robes and palms of light,
   Assembled amid the zephyrs there,
To witness the wedding
   Of this enamored pair.

While Cupid with his bow
Kept running to and fro,

Shooting silvered arrows keen,
In mere wantonness of joy,
   At the love god and his queen.

Then the celestial company,
Chanting loudly, chanting lowly,
   With heavenly eye intent,
Went upward winging
   Into the blue element.

Eros and the maid
Took it as an omen ill of evil aid,
   That Cupid should play such pranks,
While they stood plighted
   On the river's sacred banks.

Said the maiden Mildred then,
"Thou god of angels and of men,
   Though I worship thee,
This surely doth portend
   Our marriage would be merged in misery.

"Oh, I fear that I
   Should meet the displeasure of the sky;
   And that undying as thou art
The dews of death
   Would settle 'round thy heart.

"'Tis better that you go
  To lands of light where never winds doth blow;
    But I beg of thou
  One heavenly kiss at parting,
    To cool the fever in my brow."

The god amazed
In silence on her gazed,
  And simply said,
After the parting kiss
  On her forehead had been laid:

"My Mildred, dear, adieu.
  I'll wait on the river's farther strand for you,
    And have the boatman pale,
  When thou art coming,
    Signal on the gale.

"I'll take you by the hand,
  And our wedding shall be witnessed by the angel band;
    I'll lead you on the streets of gold
  To a mansion ready made,
    That time shall never mould.

"And throughout the days
  Of duration's endless maze,
    Our love on earth begun

Shall changeless be
　　As the brightness of the sun."

He waived adieu,
And in the parting blue,
　　Oh, rapturous sight!
Mildred saw her lover
　　Lost in supernal light.

Long she standing gazed,
With eye upraised,
　　Entranced at the heavenly sound
Which came floating
　　Like a song of glory 'round.

The chorus died away,
And Mildred went her homeward way;
　　But on the river's strand
The fishermen ofttimes
　　See her stand,

With hand upraised,
As if in silence still she gazed
　　Into the ether blue,
For some lost image
　　To fall upon her view.

TWO ANGELS.

I.

In pensive mood,
Through a lighted wood,
In meditation bent,
Following a golden butterfly,
I musing went;
When the night was setting in,
And the moon and stars
Like crystal bars
Lit up the firmament.

II.

I followed my little guide,
Thither I knew not where,
Like a golden glory fair,
Near a rugged mountain wild and wide,
Along a mute brookside,
Meandering silently
Onward to an illumined sea,
Whose banks shown bright
With rarest light,

While doves and pelicans
Sported there in glee.

III.

Along its silver'd shore,
I followed my guide once more,
Through the verdant bloom
Of blushing flowers,
Whose sweet perfume
Turns to heaven
This world of ours.

IV.

In fairest rank,
On either bank,
Palm trees stood in line,
Whose leafy shade
And waving made
A canopy divine;
Where love might stray
In listless mood,
Dreaming life away
With the heavenly sisterhood.

V.

The celestial asphodels
And heathery hairbells

Nodded in the breeze;
The lark and linnet too,
Nested in the trees,
Undisturbed by hawk or hound,
In the midst of that sweet Eden
Which my little guide had found.

VI.

Resting on a rose's stem,
It bade me drink
From the brimming brink,
By silent sign
Like messenger divine,
Plain as word of men.

VII.

O the water free
Gave new life to me,
While I did lave
My face and hands
In its sacred wave.

VIII.

Then I knew
Some shape of heavenly hue,
Just out of the boundless blue,
Must linger there
Within that Eden fair.

IX.

Then I seen,
O fair, celestial sight!
By the radiant light
Of a heavenly gleam,
Two lovely angels that
On a structure rude
Under a palm tree sat,
Between the lake and wood.

X.

One was gentle, mild,
With beauty's charms, undefiled,
Whose golden hair
And form so fair
Spoke her of the gentle sect
Heavenly and circumspect.

XI.

The other kind
Had a sterner mind,
Moved less by danger,
Less by love;
But more at the fall
From friendship's all
Of a fainting dove.

XII.

He spoke to her
Like a worshiper
From yonder sky
With a celestial light
Kindling in his eye.

XIII.

They sung a strain
That woke a flame
Of love within my soul,
Which never will burn dim
As the ages flitting swim
Through eternity's goal.

XIV.

The raptures of that line,
The music all divine,
The seraphic spell,
Into my soul's center fell.

XV.

The chorus through,
The angels flew
Straight into heaven
Beyond my view.
Hand in hand they went,

With faces upward bent,
In a maze of light,
On which I stood and gazed
Through half the night.

XVI.

Whereat some magic seemed
To change the garden
Where I dreamed
Into a wilderness dim,
Whose flowerets faded
'Round the water's rim;
And the butterfly bright
Changed his wings of light
To an insect grim,
Which did my soul affright,
And a darksome shade
Strode over the glade,
Casting a chill
On lake and hill,
Like the mists
Of a freezing rill.

XVII.

Whereat he spoke
In gruffest voice to me,
As if something in his throat

Was chuckling there to see
A human shape,
On which to gloat eternally:

XVIII.

"'Tis well I found the way,
Running so near to heaven
And yet astray;
But let it pass,
Ere this day sever,
My friends and me
Have a feast to hold
On thy body cold,
Wasting to mold
When the last bell's tolled."

XIX.

He said no more,
But a cave on shore
Swallowed him then
From my affrighted ken,
While I seemed to feel
The prod of a pointed steel,
Piercing with pain
My very brain.
In the dizzy gloom
A fainting swoon

Felled me to the earth,
Amid the tyrant's mirth.
As his voice rang through the sky:
" Thus and thus
Shall every mortal die."

ANNALEE.

One lovely night in June,
When nature's harp was all atune,
I wandered o'er a distant glade,
Arm in arm with a beauteous maid,
Methought so sinless and so fair,
Naught on earth with her could compare.
She seemed a seraph, sent
From heaven's high battlement,
To be my earthly guide,
O'er this waste so wild and wide.

Hand in hand we wandered on
O'er the fragrant, flowery lawn.
Gentle zephyrs cooling came,
Stirring thoughts within my brain —
Thoughts of bliss and heaven, to be
Passed in pleasure with my darling Annalee;
Sheltered on some fairy shore,
Where summer blooms forevermore;
Where life's wild tumult and care,
Ne'er enters that sinless shelter fair,

To mar the blooming brow of bloom
With shades of sorrow,
Darker than the tomb,
With drapery dismal as death weaves
Around the reaper's falling sheaves;
Where healing springs so clear,
Purify the crystal atmosphere;
Where the silver-headed swain
Gets his earthly gain
By grazing flocks that feed
On the heather and the mead;
And all the rustic neighbors are
Loving in my fancy's fairy island far.

Her tender accents mild and sweet,
My listening ear did greet,
As we tripped adown the mountain
To a cool and shady fountain,
Near whose silvery rilled expanse
We passed the morning moments of existence.
Seated on a rustic structure near,
We seemed the cupids all to hear
Lisping notes so sweet in rhyme,
That all the moving leaves did chime
A serenade to my queen so fair,
Throughout the musical murmuring air.

The moonbeam's glowing light
Cast a halo round our dreamy sight,
Tingeing with a golden foliage new
All nature's veiled and varied hue,
Lighting like celestial beam
Our lifetime's morning scene;
Rearing crystal castles bright,
Where all the day and night
Of time, no shadow would stalk
Across our favorite winding walk,
To cast a chill within our cottage door
On my fancy's fairy island shore.

Her loving face upturned to mine
Seemed then to be all but divine,
As I gazed beyond control
Down through the windows of her soul;
Within that leafy shade
And peaceful colonnade,
Beyond earth's care and dole.
Wrapt in meditative thought,
What strange emotions in me wrought,
As we pledged our lives away,
With words I cannot say;
As we bound our souls to be
Each other's through all eternity.

Then we broke a piece of gold,
As in the far-off days of old,
For a simple token to recall
The moment we gave away our all;
And with a silken ribbon blue
She hung it on her neck and bosom too,
And bade me keep the other part
Till on life's eternal mart
We should meet full in sight
Of the celestial city's light;
There in rapture's sweetest sway
To pass love's never-ending day.

We left the fountain and the hill,
Homeward wending near a silvery rill,
Whose mingling murmurs came,
Ever ladened with her name,
On the dream-like breezes swell
Throughout that peaceful dell,
To me a blissful Eden fair,
For the angel of my life was there.

We parted at the gate
Of her father's house of state,
With hopes beaming bright,
With hearts all life and light;

With a golden, glorious day
Dawning just beyond the horizon's gray.

But alas! three suns had hardly sped
When my darling Annalee was dead.
Her saintly soul had gone
From darkness up to dawn,
Away amid the starry spheres,
There to stay through endless years.

The cruel archer with his bow
Had taken her over the wave of woe.
Away from the fountain and the hill,
Away from the silvery rippling rill,
Away from this heart of mine;
Where I might not twine,
One garland fair
About her angel forehead there.

ORPHEUS AND EURYDICE.

Once a wight of the olden time,
Who lived in a sunny clime,
As some of the poets tell,
Took a midnight trip to hell,
In hopes to find his missing wife,
The comfort and the scourge of all his life.
Her name was Eurydice,
She had been married twice;
His was Orpheus,
And not much behind her in a fuss.

Philosophizing there
   Where they were wed—
This ill-united pair—
   Thus to himself he said:

"She must be in the land
   Bordering on the devil's strand,
For the Lord of earth and air
Would'nt have her there,
Knowing of her tongue

Which in this ear hath rung,
Till there is'nt left
The vestige of a drum.
But I must find this mate,
That she may one day prate
Over my body lying in state,
When the spirit's gone
To those mansions of glory
Building in the land of song."

He downward wends his way,
Journeying wondrous gay,
Like a lark at morn
Singing all the way.

The reason would'st thou know,
She was'nt at his elbow,
Nor yet beside him—
Or the poets have belied him.

Through those vistas green,
Where shades and shadows intervene,
As he passed along,
There danced a merry throng
To the music of his song;
As on Afric's sunny plains
I've heard immortal fiddler's strains

Captivate the wondering swains,
And make them circling go
Like dudes and dandies in a row.

To Pluto's court he came.
Where peering through the flame,
Ten thousand horrid eyes
Lit up the lambent skies;
But gathering up his cheer
He faltered forth in fear,
"Is my lost wife here?"

The listening imps around
Laughed with mimic sound,
At the question odd and queer,
"Is my lost wife here;"
Up spoke the leader of them all:
"Hearken to the words that fall;
This must a mortal madman be;
Brother fiends we're happier far than he:
For who'd torment his eye,
In these regions deep,
With one tearful sigh
Such wife to keep."

But mournful still,
With supplicating will,

His suit he urges well,
Like the sounding knell
Of a funeral bell,
When some lost soul
Goes speeding to its goal,
Over the Stygian tide,
Into the realm of mystery wide.

He soothes with wily art
The monarch's hardened heart,
And lulls his piercing pain,
And gets his lost wife back again.

"Speak no further word,"
　Grim Pluto cries,
"Thy prayer is heard—
On this condition take thy prize:
Turn not thine eyes
On her form beside thee there;
For this I vow,
The instant thou
My parting word denies,
She vanishes in mid air."

Up the strange ascent,
Orpheus as ordered
Foremost went;

Though when two mortals
Leave their sphere,
And downward steer,
The man, as most befitting,
Follows in the rear.
As up and on they sped,
The foolish fool turned 'round his head;
That instant in mid air,
His Eurydice was fled.

If it was by
Some angel of the sky,
All purposely designed,
He hath much cause
To be resigned;
Or if by chance the spell,
No mortal tongue may tell
The good fortune
That Orpheus there befell.

'Tis true he journeyd home
The remaining way alone,
And missed his Eurydice
Some once or twice.
But then he lived in peace,
Tending his flocks and geese,
Reading the word divine

Under the spreading leaves
Of his trellised vine,
Embowered in light the while,
Thrown from the glowing portals
Of the far-off, heavenly isle,
Till his latest sun went down,
Without one fret or frown
From his missing Eurydice
To thrill or chill
His heart like ice.

ST. PETER AT THE GATE.

A traveler on the heavenly highway,
Journeying near the gate of gold,
Thus accosted St. Peter one day
With look so very bold:
"Why keepest thou this gate
Encompassed 'round so close,
Where many wanderers wait
To gain the heavenly land perforce?"

St. Peter made reply
In mild, submissive mood,
Echoed through the sky
By the heavenly sisterhood:
"My task hath been
These centuries old
To shut out sinful men
From the shepherd's fold.
This golden gate
I instant close,
By the decrees of fate,

On just Alla's foes
Who wander this way late."

Thus the celestial traveler again:
"I lost my way, and went astray
On some miry plain,
Which caused delay;
But then I ran
With all my speed
O'er stock and stone,
Past many a man
On heathery mead,
Pausing only to read,
In the twilight fine,
Each word and line
Of the apostles' creed.
With vanishing haste,
Like a winged steed,
I skimmed the waste;
Seeking to be
A timely guest
In heaven's festivity,
With the good and blest.
Then let me in,
St. Peter, do!
It would be sin

To shut from me
That glimpse of glory;
For I've been told
The angel's story
About those streets of gold,
And that heavenly land,
With mountains grand
And hoary.   I come alone.
It would be sin
To spurn me from the throne.

"The night is cold and chill,
My limbs are stiff with age;
I've clambered up life's hill
Without a staff or page;
Then let one golden ray of glory
Break gently through
On this pilgrim old and hoary,
Oh, St. Peter, do!"

The crystal bar
All motionless remained,
And a stillness far
Throughout heaven reigned—
Till St. Peter made reply:
"'Tis not thine to behold
The glories of the sky.

Go wander away
From the gate of gold,
And paths where angels stray;
'Tis the fates' decree.
Mountain barriers lie
Between heaven and thee,
Which thou mayest not climb,
To the land of bliss sublime."

He turned him away
From the gate of gold,
And took the lonely way
Down to the nether wold,
Leading where so many fall,
Missing God, and heaven, and all.

THE LAND OF LOVE.

They tell of a land of love,
All radiant and bright above,
Where shining seraph wings
Keep time to the rhyme its people sings;
Chanting in angelic lays
Holy Alla's endless praise.

They tell of a city of bliss,
Located far from this,
Where no discordant word
Ever yet was heard
Amid that celestial air
Spoken by the shining fair,
Who ever and ever flit
'Round where the gods in grandeur sit,
Waving wreaths of beauteous evergreen,
Pluck'd from some sylvan scene
Within Eden's olive shades
By sinless, sainted maids.

They tell of golden gleaming streets
Where earth and heaven meets;

Where glowing towers of light
Fall on the celestial wanderer's sight;
Where limpid streams are flowing,
Ever from Alla's throne going,
Carrying mellow mercy on their tide;
Throughout the land they glide,
Meandering thitherward away
From the fount of eternal day.

They tell of a fabled spring,
Near which little cherubs sing
Notes of soul-subduing bliss,
All blending most harmonious;
Poured from purity's fount,
Higher and higher they mount,
Till the happy, angelic throng
Catch the soul of song
And echo the chorus loud and long.

They tell of a lucid lake
Where all admitted souls take
Their first, fond draught of joy.
Deep they drink without alloy
Of that eternal pool—
Soul-cleansing and cool—
Upon whose banks there be
Amber bowls of purity,

Sparkling like the gleam
Of bright jewels beneath the stream.

They tell of golden-fruited trees,
Which sway in heaven's ambrosial breeze,
Alluring the gods of bliss to wait;
Where beauteous angels congregate
To chant their endless lay
With those heavenly choristers
That thitherward stray.

They tell of a golden gate,
Near which loving angels wait
To welcome in with holy song,
And praises loud and long,
Those who kept the shining way
Upward to the fount of day.

They tell of a winding stair
Leading to a scene so fair
That naught on earth can be
Found of sufficient purity
To make the steps, o'er which ever go
Infant feet from this world of woe.

They tell of a distant place
Where loving angels chase

Away those wicked spirits,
Whose deathly touch blights
The sinless soul's angelic hue
Darkly through and through.

They tell of an Eden land
Where this human band
Will be crowned all beautiful,
For being ever dutiful;
Where sorrow may not come
When the heavenly anthem's begun.
And no beggar, begging bread,
On that golden floor will tread
To jar the chords of bliss,
Tuned most harmonious;
Where day and night will be,
Beyond that crystal sea,
Changeless to all eternity.

MISCELLANEOUS POEMS.

LIFE'S BATTLES.

Do you wish to gain
    The battles of your life?
Then press boldly onward
    To its deadliest strife.

Should they be fierce and bloody,
    Fight them with a vim;
Pressing onward to victory:
    For valiantry will win.

Bravely battling with courage,
    Life's barriers will fall;
And you'll conquer in the fight,
    Be the foeman great or small.

Let the monitor within
    Ever guide you in the fray;
With duty as your countersign
    You'll never go astray.

With hope upon your helmet
    And right upon your side,

You may march to victory,
   Casting consternation wide.

Onward strive and upward;
   Be a leader in the van,
Remember fire proves the metals
   As trials do the man.

Then buckle on your armor
   And grasp the cutlass keen,
Blinding your enemy
   With the shimmer of its sheen.

Let no phantom daunt you,
   And never failure fear;
Striking boldly for the prize
   Which glimmers bright and near.

Should you faintness feel
   From exchanging blows,
Remember that courage
   Will daunt the bravest foes;

That manhood mailed in right,
   With the banner of God unfurled,
Will conquer in the strife,
   In the face of all the world.

Then strike for the victory,
    For the crowning act of life
Is to walk triumphantly
    From the world's battle and strife,

Upward to creation's mead,
    Where sunlight eternal shines
Effulgent and resplendently,
    Along destiny's distant lines.

BRAVE-BORN SOULS.

"Fortune favors the brave,"
    While cowards sit sulking
On the stones of their grave;
    Victory's banner may gleam,
While life's drowsy dreamers
    Go sailing down its stream.

The eagle of happiness screams,
Bathed in the sunlight
Of visions and dreams;
    While the night owl of gloom
Mopes moodily round
    Some old, ivied ruin of the tomb.

The shout of a soul that's free,
Drinking draughts of bliss
From the fount of purity,
   Will move the angel band
More than the chorus
   Of ten thousand drones of the land.

He who bridges some Alpine crest
With mind or matter's motion,
Making an escape way for the oppressed,
Over time's extended ocean,
Doth more for the race of man
Than the rulers of Cuba or Japan.

He who points to Calvary's height
When the glow is darkest,
May cheer the fainting wight
   More than the sunshine saint
Who, on the brink of perils point,
   Will shrink and faint.

Then strike a blow
That will somewhere tell
On friend or foe,
   Rather than stand
Guide-boards of folly
   In this favored land.

For battles must be fought
And victories must be won;
And in the book of life we're taught
  That the hidden talent gave
No passport to its owner,
  Who had a soul to save.

It were better to be
Far fathoms deep
Under the earth and sea,
  Than loiter about in the way
Of the immortal masters,
  Marching to the judgment day.

THERE IS NO UNBELIEF.

There is no unbelief:
Whoever plants a seed
  Beneath the sod,
On the heather or the mead,
  Trusts in God;
E'en though he be of sinners chief,
'Tis plain he hath belief.

There is no unbelief:
Whoever says, when clouds obscure the sky:

"Be patient, thou,
'Twill brighten by and by!"
   God's mercy doth avow;
E'en though he be of sinners chief,
'Tis plain he hath belief.

There is no unbelief:
Whoever sees, neath winter's snow,
   The working of a power
Which makes the daisy grow,
   Owns God every hour;
E'en though he be of sinners chief,
'Tis plain he hath belief.

There is no unbelief:
Whoever lieth down to sleep
   Upon the land or billow,
Trusteth God to safely keep
   His head on nature's pillow;
E'en though he be of sinners chief,
'Tis plain he hath belief.

There is no unbelief:
Whoever speaks of "the coming morn,"
   Or "the vast unknown,"
Hath been heavenly born—
   For these are the Lord's alone;

E'en though he be of sinners chief,
'Tis plain he hath belief.

There is no unbelief:
Whoever looks on death
   When the eyelids close,
And keepeth still his breath,
   God's kindness knows;
E'en though he be of sinners chief,
'Tis plain he hath belief.

There is no unbelief:
At morn when man awakes,
   A glimpse of God's glory
His soul unconsciously takes
   From mountains old and hoary;
E'en though he be of sinners chief,
'Tis plain he hath belief.

There is no unbelief:
Whoever dreams of life,
   In another land
Beyond this mortal strife,
   Obeyeth God's command;
E'en though he be of sinners chief,
'Tis plain he hath belief.

HOW A LARK CHEERED A DROOPING SOUL.

The sun was darkly hid,
   One dull November day;
The snow fell fast and cold,
   As a traveler strayed from home away.

Forced to face the storm
   That his children might be fed;
He wandered on in gloomy mood,
   Like one who walks among the dead.

Tired, soul-sick, and aweary
   Of that which men call life,
So he held this mental conflict,
   "Would he use the suicidal knife?"

"What cheer for me hath earth,
   Toiling on starvation pay,
With loved ones ragged and poor?
   I'll end this life to-day."

Just then he heard the merry tune
   Of a lark upon a bough,
Caroled joyful in the storm,
   Which lit his troubled brow.

HOW A LARK CHEERED A DROOPING SOUL.

The little lark sang gaily on,
   Though blown with winds so rude;
And this was the burden of his song:
   "Be cheerful, God is good."

In silence then the traveler stood,
   Listening the song to hear;
It thrilled his being through,
   And filled his soul with cheer.

He fell upon his knees
   And thanked the God of heaven there;
And never before did the winds
   Bear upward such a prayer.

He rose and hailed the little songstress
   As an omen bright of hope,
For cheering his drooping heart
   To go into the world with men to cope.

The God of heaven favored him
   With stores of goodly grain;
His children were well fed,
   And sheltered from the rain.

Oh, ye drooping souls,
   Be cheered by the song of birds!

For their warbled music
   Is set to heavenly words.

The hand that guides the storm
   Sheltered the little bird from death;
Then toil thou bravely on,
   And praise Him with thy latest breath.

FLAKES OF SNOW.

Flakes of snow, flakes of snow,
Falling on the world below,
Pure, white, spotless, free,
From the shrine of divinity;
Soft as an angel's touch,
White as the forms we worship much,
Who have climbed the golden stair
And gone to a land so very fair,
From the snow, from the snow.

Flakes of snow, flakes of snow!
Oh, whither dost thou go,
When the gentle summer rain
Bids the back to heaven again?
And what touch of angel hands

Forms thee new for other lands,
With thy coat of spotless white,
Like the radiance of an eternal light,
Breaking on the snow, on the snow?

Flakes of snow, flakes of snow,
Fair as the tinted rainbow,
Falling near and far
From nature's fairy car,
Drawn by steeds of light
Though the dome of duration bright,
Moved at Neptune's will
With the speed of a lightening thrill,
Above the snow, above the snow.

Flakes of snow, flakes of snow,
Where you fall no grass doth grow,
No warbling bird doth tune
Its silvery cadence to the moon.
King Frost triumphant reigns,
Bound in winter's icy chains,
Like the shadow of a fate,
Mirrored on the tomb where all must wait
'Neath the snow, 'neath the snow.

Flakes of snow, flakes of snow,
Borne on eternity's silent flow,

Ye sadly call to mind
The faces I've left behind,
The severed ties and troubled fears
Buried 'neath the weight of years,
For a deep, brooding silence reigns,
When ye fleck with white the plains
Over with snow, over with snow.

Flakes of snow, flakes of snow,
When my work is done below,
May I sink to slumber
With God's chosen number,
Pure as the snowy plain;
And when Gabriel's bugle strain
Calls buried millions to the light,
Oh, may I wear a vesture just as white
As the snow, as the snow.

THE ORDERLY'S RIDE.

Thundering o'er the highway,
　Clattering down the ridge,
Rode in haste a rider
　Over the burning bridge
Fired by rebel brands,

Above the torrent's flow,
Rolling onward to the ocean,
   With murmur soft and low.

The steed was flecked with foam,
   He staggered and gasped for breath,
As he bore his rider from the foe
   Onward to the marl of death;
In hard and hot pursuit
   Nine angry rebels rode,
'Twere death to flee, and death to stand;
   On every hand bright bayonets glowed.

Along the bridge they sped,
   'Midst flame and smoke,
When from the friendly shore
   A shout of "courage" broke.
But see! the bridge is swaying,
   The loosened timbers fall;
And headlong into the waters
   Plunge the horse and rider all.

The faithful steed was killed,
   The gallant rider drowned
'Neath the mighty debris,
   Which cracked like an earthquake's sound.
Meanwhile the battle rolled

Throughout that dreadful day,
But victory came in the eventide
Where the dead and dying lay.

The horse was seen no more;
By the light of the moonbeam cold
They found the rider crushed and dead,
With a message to Grant in his dying hold:
"The rebels are moving,
Prepare for attack;
They've gained the road;
Send no message back."

For six long miles
The orderly flew,
At his commander's will,
Mounted on steed so true;
Pursued, hemmed in, cut off,
But somehow he hastened on,
To a death of terrible doom
And the judgment dawn.

'Neath the light of the stars,
And the sound of the sentry's tread,
They scooped a hasty place
For his burial bed;
Then they said a short prayer,

And moistened with tears the sod,
And left him to the vigils of time
And eternity's God.

EVENTIDE IN THE RHINELAND.

In the bright, beautiful Rhineland,
   When one golden day was ending,
And the odorous vineland
   Was with purple clusters bending,
   And the western sun his light was lending;
I saw her then in the eventide
My bonnie, brown-eyed bride,
   It was the first time we met—
Me and my Melo Clide.
   Oh, I see that vision yet!

She was standing all alone,
   Mid light of her own making;
Singing with softly tender tone,
   As the aspen leaves were shaking,
   And the soul's deep current waking.
The river ran beside her feet,
Oh, her voice was tender, sweet!
   I gazed and gazed my heart away,

In the sunny Rhineland's retreat,
   On the eve of that declining day.

A golden glory filled the air,
   Lighting all the lovely scene,
Tinging her rich auburn hair
   With a celestial gleam,
   Breaking from heaven's court supreme;
The drowsy humming bee,
The restless rooks upon the lea,
   And the lark, uprising, gave
A shadow of sublimity
   To mountain, meadow, wave.

The distant shepherd's bell,
   The mournful monk at prayer,
On my dreamy ear fell
   While I stood pondering there
   Of the Rhineland maiden fair;
And believe me, on my word,
Methought somehow I heard
   Cupid gently calling then,
With voice which instant stirred
   Sylvan shadows in the glen.

Upon her mirage in the stream
   She gazed with smiles and blushes,

In a sort of seraph dream,
   As the water kissed the rushes,
   Startling the timid thrushes;
Then she took an arrow from her hair
Which fell about her shoulders fair,
   And threw it with a little start
In playful mood upon the air;
   Its silvery keenness pierced my heart.

AWAY TO-NIGHT.

Away to-night,
Away from home and friends,
While the light
In the tear-dimmed sight
Glimmers, and flickers, and blends;
And faces strange
Meet my glance,
With look askance
As on I range,
In a sort of trance.

The world seems cold
As hoarded gold,
When lambs go wandering from the fold,

And shepherds grow
More gruff and grim,
When the sun is low
Near the horizon's rim,
If they must seek
The fondlings strayed,
Over mountains bare and bleak.

MIDNIGHT ON THE BATTLE FIELD.

'Tis midnight on the battle field,
The wind's low moan is chill,
Our army's on the march again,
After the battle of Chancellorsville;
The drum's slow beat
And weary feet
Tell of courage tried;
Brave souls, of honor born,
Their manly leader's pride.

The moonbeam's silvery gleam
Gilds with beauty that marl of death;
Hushed and silent now,
Is the angry foeman's breath;
All peaceful, still,

MIDNIGHT ON THE BATTLE FIELD.

They slumber on the hill,
While the sentinel stars above
Look down in sorrow,
From seraph lands of love.

The prowling cat and hungry wolf
Have gathered on the mead,
They tear anew, in heaven's view,
Wounds of death that bleed;
Their famished jaws
And angry claws
Tear with a sensation sore
Flesh from the fairest form
A mother ever bore.

The sinless angels of the sky
Shudder such sights to see,
While some soldier's soul
Goes speeding away to the realms of eternity;
Alone in the darkness there,
Grown frantic with despair,
Some slowly-dying soul
Struggles the burial clods
From his bosom to roll.

Thus the cheerless night went by,
And the misty morning gray

Broke up in the dull sky,
Where the dead and dying lay;
While all along the line
Some shattered pine,
Or strong oaken hold,
Grim tales of war
Their story told.

SITTING AT THE STILE.

I'm sitting at the stile, Mary,
    Waiting now for you,
While the moonbeams glimmer on the grass
    With a glorious, golden hue.
The merry lark is singing
    Like a herald of the morn,
And the drowsy beetle flits,
    While I linger here forlorn.

The stars of heaven shine, Mary,
    And softly twinkle 'round,
The rippling rills go murmuring
    Love's sweet, seraph sound.
Some mystic presence seems
    Sent by Cupid's care

SITTING AT THE STILE.

To dim the brightness of my life
   With the shadow of despair.

Why sit I at the stile, Mary,
   Since you so fickle proved,
And went off with another
   Whose soul is more coarsely grooved;
Thoughtless of the anguish
   Thou didst waken in my heart,
Thrilling through its center,
   Like a deadly, poisoned dart.

I linger at the stile, Mary,
   Because of the hope you bore,
When fancy's fairy argos
   Landed at love's shore,
In the May-day of our spring,
   As we builded castles fair,
By the light of soft, celestial tapers,
   Burning brightly in the air.

That vision's sped away, Mary,
   And I think it cruel, too,
That those shining castles fell
   Because thou wert untrue;
For the heart that once
   Hath sipped from love's bowl,

That sweet, delicious draught
    Will move to madness the soul.

I wait and watch for thee, Mary,
    Through the long and dreary nights,
And ofttimes see thee coming
    In my imagination's sights;
As the angels, silken shod,
    Waft their velvet wings,
Around the orient's golden crest,
    When the curfew vesper rings.

In the other world, Mary,
    Beyond the crystal sea,
If the light of thine eye
    Falls not kindly on me,
And if there is no stile
    Where I may waiting stay,
The rays of eternal brightness,
    Will fall cheerless on my way.

OUR SLEEPING DEAD.

Softly step and lightly tread,
For on those southern grounds
Lie buried now the nation's dead;

OUR SLEEPING DEAD.

Beneath the tangled grass
In the deep morass,
In each silent nook we pass,
Some comrade true,
Who wore the army blue,
Lies sleeping now the sleep of death,
Under the daisies and the dew.

The running rill
Or moaning wind,
Past mount or hill,
Breaks not the spell
Which 'round those sleepers dwell,
On open plain, or in secluded dell,
Who neglected there hath lain
Since freedom's sons, and union guns,
Broke slavery's cruel chain.
On the outmost post
Of Columbia's coast;
To celestial music
March our maimed and murdered host,
Led by Lincoln's soul,
Through lands of light they stroll
All noiselessly away,
To the bright camping grounds
Of eternal day.

Oh, let them sleep
Through the ages still,
As the winds of eternity sweep
Down creation's hill;
Till the herald of morn shall fly,
Calling those sleepers
To the encampment of the sky,
From their cold retreat
To the bliss and glory
Of the golden street.

HOPE ON.

Hope on, hope ever,
Yield to fate never;
For beyond the dim hills
Glows the paradise light forever.

Beyond the darkness and gloom,
Beyond the dim isles of the tomb,
Angels bright, heavenly, stray,
Through fragrance and flowery perfume.

And, standing there, sings
Hope the bright angel with glittering wings

Melodies fine,
Of heaven and heavenly things.

On that bright shore,
When life's battles are o'er,
Fate with his fearless frown
Shall be seen nevermore.

In that fair land of bloom,
No raven of gloom
Or shadowy phantom
Flits 'round the tomb.

But angels of light,
With crowns fair and bright,
Everywhere meet
The celestial wanderer's sight.

From harp strings of gold
Soft-sounding anthems are rolled,
More mellow and rare
Than mortal e'er told.

And Peris divine,
In the celestial light's shine,
In attitudes bow
'Round Alla's bright shrine;

While meandering go
Silvered rivers aglow
With the paradise light,
In one eternal flow.

Then ever hope on,
Through darkness and dawn,
For the celestial harp strings
Vibrate with heavenly song.

And never despair
When the hearth-stone's bare,
For the sunshine of life
Glows bright over there.

BURIED YEARS.

Buried years,
Full of tears,
Full of hopes and fears,
Lost in the gulf of time;
Still we hear your dying chime,
Like a silver thread,
Or a weight of lead
Sounding from the coffined dead.

Quick you went,
And were spent
Like a flash in the firmament;
But a lingering gleam
Like a meteor's sheen,
Breaking amid silvery spray,
Flashes back to-day
Joys as you sped away.

Still lingers yet
Some fond regret,
Where kindred met;
Before fate's band
Sailed past eternity's strand,
Carrying away
Through the river's spray
The lonely widow's stay.

From the gulf of time,
Deep and sublime,
Echoes back your dying chime;
As year by year,
Fled past us here,
Scarce missed till gone,
Like dews upon the lawn,
Vanished in the early dawn.

Thou hast flown
Into the unknown,
Numbered by the Lord alone;
For some purpose grand
We may not understand;
But still there comes,
With the receding suns,
Sad memories, like muffled drums.

Commoners and peers,
As eternity nears,
Regret those buried years;
But they cannot call
One moment back, though small,
In which to right
The soul all pure and bright
For its eternal flight.

Away from earth,
From joy and mirth,
Beyond the mystic birth;
Where man shall stand
On the shores of the heavenly land,
To receive his doom
For the lake of gloom,
Or regions bright with bloom.

MABEL MAY.

Dwelt a lonely cotter
   In a secluded way,
Who had an only daughter,
   Named Mabel May.

Her face was very fair,
   And her eyes of liquid light
Shown like an angel's rare
   Viewed in the northern night.

She was nature's child,
   Reared among the mountain herds
And ptarmigan wild;
   Of few and loving words.

She fished in the fairest streams,
   With an amber hook,
Which shot its brightest gleams
   Into every darkened nook.

And oft in nature's hush,
   When no sound was stirring
Save the speckled thrush
   Or the woodpecker's burring,

I've heard her tune
   Her talking timbrel
To the laughing moon,
   On the balmy breeze's swell.

And once as she sang
   Some selected line,
The hills resounding rang
   With the chorus all divine.

Angels were in waiting,
   Though unseen, around,
And they joined in making
   The chorus more profound.

A soft, celestial ray
   Falling from the gate of gold
Broke brightly 'round Mabel May,
   In that wooded wold.

Two forms arrayed in white,
   Shining and so fair,
Climbed the azure height,
   With Mabel between them there.

By her grave 'neath the willow tree
   Ofttimes mournful sits

Her father wearily,
    As the darkening daylight flits.

On a stone of fairest marble,
    Carved with skill and care,
Reads "Our darling Mabel
    Sings with the shining fair."

And remembrance dear,
    Winging in silence away,
Ofttimes sheds a tear
    For the lovely Mabel May.

NO EARTHLY VOICE.

While crossing a lonely wold
    One dark and dismal night,
I met a madman crippled and old,
    Whom I took for the devil's sprite.
His form was lank and long,
    His face was haggard and wan;
And the burden of his song
    Was, "Help me if you can."

"What wouldst thou have," said I,
    "That I can now bestow?"

He leered, with the light of hell in his eye,
    And said, "Mercy from below."
"From that dread domain,
    Or its ruler with heartless heart,
No mercy can you gain:
    Then tell me what thou art."

He spoke with a weird and woeful wail:
    "Look away off' yonder in the air,
Where the wind whirls wild in a frisky gale;
    'Twas there I prayed my last prayer,
And sold my soul for the devil's toll,
    That the mills of God might grind a man;
Then help me if you can."

I left the barren moor;
    I left the green sea lea;
I ran as I never run before,
    For that shape of hell was after me.
I could hear his clattering stride
    And feel his panting breath;
He was running at my side
    The race of life and death.

I ran, I flew, with hair on end,
    I ran a brooklet through,
And this the charm dispelled:

For I never saw him more.
And I never crossed the wold amain;
I ran till I reached my cottage door.
But oft, in seeming, I've run that race again.

NEARING THE END.

Over the hill-tops of life,
    Down into the valley we wend;
Growing more aged and gray,
    Soon to separate, comrade and friend.

We who fought to the death
    In the years long ago:
Those who shot at the flag,
    And made us their foe.

Since the last battle, my comrades,
    Since the Union was saved,
Time has been silvering our hairs,
    Like the sheen of the wave.

Since those rebel prison pens
    Barred in such dreadful woes,
Many surviving comrades have gone
    To meet our Union's foes;

Who madly fought and fell,
   In the fearful crash and strife
Of a grand and mighty nation
   Struggling for union and for life.

Many a soldier has been placed at rest
   Since Johnson and since Lee
Laid down their arms
   In the face of earth and Deity.

Over on the celestial parade ground,
   Beyond this world's hem,
We may meet and recognize
   Those misguided men.

For soon the death angel will come,
   As near to the valley we wend,
Seeking the aged and gray,
   And all who are nearing the end.

Old army boys so true,
   Who rallied at the call:
Time is thinning out our ranks,
   Soon the last must fall.

But wherever it may be,
   Under whatever sky,

On the fair, bright shore
   We'll gather by and by.

For beyond the dim hills
   Glows the bright light of life,
Where the soldier may bivouac
   Safe from all strife.

Where comrade and where friend,
   Nevermore shall part
Throughout the endless ages
   Of eternity's chart.

DEATH AND THE FAIRY FAY.

Once a fairy fay
   Held in my heart command;
Her winsome smiles, na, na,
   I could not withstand.

But Death led her away
   With his icy hand,
In her morning of May,
   From this earthly strand.

I don't know the way,
   Whether by sea or land,

They journeyed that day
   Over the golden sand.

For I scarcely can say
   That I rightly understand
Whence they did stray,
   At our Lord's command.

Or what welcome gay
   She received from the angel band;
Where saints and patriarchs gray,
   Round the shrine of glory stand.

For the brightness of the ray,
   And the mystic wand,
Obscure my mental sway,
   As to what doth there portend.

THE PARADISE LIGHT.

Over the river,
Beyond the night,
Glitters and gleams
The paradise light.

THE PARADISE LIGHT.

Too brilliant for mortal,
Too bright to behold,
From this shoal of time
Where the winds whistle cold.

Over there, minaret
And tower sublime
Are bathed with a flow
Effulgent, divine.

There, seraphic and grand,
The radiance and gleam
Break gently around
On the bright water's sheen.

And the throne of our God
In the center doth stand,
Sinless and pure,
All sainted and grand.

Where blest Peris
In attitudes pray,
Crowned brilliant and bright
In the light of its ray.

There seraphs so fair
Cast halos around,

From turbans of glory
All loose and unbound.

There silvery apples,
On stems of bright gold,
Reflect back the ray
As onward 'tis rolled.

Aglow with this light
Are the bowers of bliss,
Where loving angels stray,
And never wander amiss.

And pilgrims that pass
Just under the rod
Are instantly changed
By the glory of God.

Over there golden cups
Lie 'round the lake,
Where admitted souls
Deep draughts of glory take;

Which throw back the glow,
Through the outermost sky,
To light the bright angels
That thitherward fly.

In yonder fair world
Vast multitudes stand,
With crowns on their foreheads,
And palms in their hand.

Waiting to welcome mortals away,
From the world and its night,
Full into the radiance
Of the paradise light.

FAIRY SHORE.

Golden gleams
From the fairy shore,
Through breaking clouds
Sometimes come streaming o'er,
To cheer the drooping soul
Amid the battle of life,
And its roar.

Toiling ever,
Toiling on,
Through daylight
And through dawn,
Those cheering gleams

Seem angel mercies
In our dreams,
Come to light the soul away
From the gloom of earth
To the gates of day.

And now and then
We seem to see
Some snowy form
From over the sea,
We used to know
When life was all aglow,
Beckoning to the fairy strand
Friends from this earthly land,
Over the distant way,
Out of darkness into day,
Which we so little understand.

N. B.—This volume will be forwarded to any address in the United States on receipt of price, $2.00.

JOHN PRESTON CAMPBELL,
ABILENE, KANSAS.

P. O. Box 163.

www.ingramcontent.com/pod-product-compliance
Lightning Source LLC
Chambersburg PA
CBHW020807230426
43666CB00007B/900